BEYOND THE RADICAL ROAD

The Memoirs of an Edinburgh Soothside Keelie

Robert P. Danskin

First published 2012
Revised 2013

Copyright © Robert Philp Danskin 2012

All rights reserved.

ISBN 978-1-291-58821-7

Printed and distributed by Lulu Inc and Amazon

Map of the 'Soothside' and picture of 'The Old Town of Edinburgh from Salisbury Crags' by J Douglas RSW courtesy of Peter Stubbs at edinphoto.co.uk

Images of St. Leonard's Hill tenements and the Mission Hut courtesy of capitalcollections.org.uk

The Radical Road is a track that skirts and runs the length of Salisbury Crags. It was given its name after it was paved in the aftermath of the Radical War of 1820, using the labour of unemployed weavers from the west of Scotland at the suggestion of Sir Walter Scott, who sympathised with their plight.

There is a popular riddle that goes:
Aroond aboot the Radical Road the Radical Rascal ran. How many Rs are in that? Tell me if you can!!
Answer = None (There is no letter R in the word THAT, of course.)

Keelie n. (Scot) 1. a kestrel 2. an urban ruffian or city dweller; especially Glasgow (Collins Dictionary)

All the world's a stage,
And all the men and women merely players;
They have their exits and their entrances,
And one man in his time plays many parts,
His acts being seven ages. At first, the infant,
Mewling and puking in the nurse's arms.
Then the whining schoolboy, with his satchel
And shining morning face, creeping like snail
Unwillingly to school. And then the lover,
Sighing like furnace, with a woeful ballad
Made to his mistress' eyebrow. Then a soldier,
Full of strange oaths and bearded like the pard,
Jealous in honour, sudden and quick in quarrel,
Seeking the bubble reputation
Even in the canon's mouth. And then the justice,
In fair round belly with good capon lined,
With eyes severe and beard of formal cut,
Full of wise saws and modern instances;
And so he plays his part. The sixth age shifts
Into the lean and slippered pantaloon,
With spectacles on nose and pouch on side;
His youthful hose, well saved, a world too wide
For his shrunk shank, and his big manly voice,
Turning again toward childish treble, pipes
And whistles in his sound. Last scene of all,
That ends this strange eventful history,
Is second childishness and mere oblivion,
Sans teeth, sans eyes, sans taste, sans everything.

(As You Like It, 2. 7. 139-167)

William Shakespeare

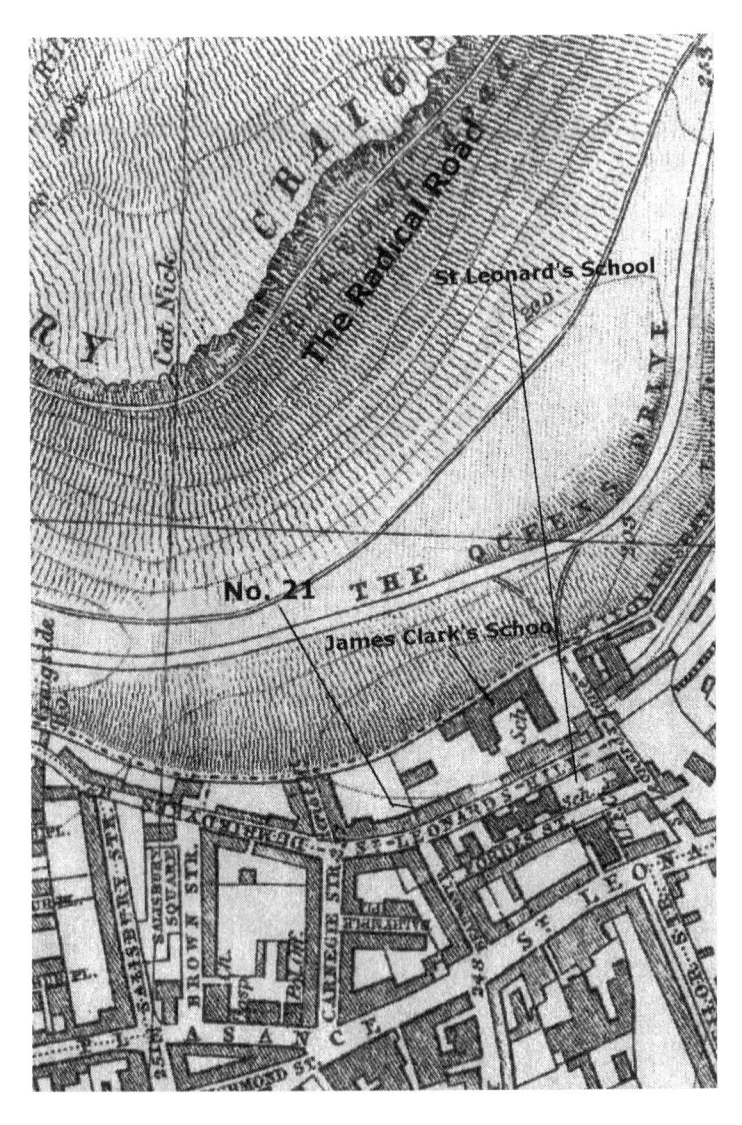

The Soothside in 1925

There was once a thriving community in Edinburgh's Soothside. It no longer exists.

For me its centre was that part of the old town, not far from Holyrood, the back street called St. Leonard's Hill. I was born in 1923 and lived there until 1932 and the memories of eighty years ago flooded back on a recent visit.

From the south side of the Hill there had been many changes. Certainly, the tenements embracing the historically named Jeanie Deans pub still stood. But my first school, St. Leonard's, its playground and jannie's cottage, had been cleared and a new building was going up on the site. Looking abandoned, the City Mission Hut stood opposite, bringing memories of the Band of Hope, the Sunday School and its seemingly tireless superintendent, Mrs Martin.

Moving on to Beaumont Place (now Bowmont), I came upon what can be described with a wee bit of exaggeration as a semi-rural scene. Where in my time there were tenements supported by shops, there were unbelievably small spaces landscaped with grass and young trees and an uninterrupted view, across the rock outcrop we called the Flaggy, to the boundary wall of Holyrood Park, The Radical Road and Salisbury Crags.

I suspect the Flaggy derived its name from the time when there was a signal station on it. We would climb up there and on to the wall, from where we had a clear view of Nelson's Monument on Calton Hill, and wait to see the black ball rise up and fall at mid-day GMT. As a bonus, at the right time of year the One-O'Clock Gun at the Castle would boom out at the same time. Perhaps there was a connection in days gone by between Calton Hill and the Flaggy, when beacons and semaphore were the standard means of long-distance communication. Anyway, the relatively few residents now living in the modern houses occupying the ground once bounded by the even-numbered tenements of Beaumont Place, St. Leonard's Hill and Carnegie St/Dalyrymple Place – all but a much reduced part of the first named remains – are fortunate to be in such a quiet and pleasant environment. A man and his dog were the only signs of life I saw. And yet two busy roads leading out of the city to the South are only a few yards away. Such a contrast to the scene as I remember it!

St. Leonard's Hill in 1959, shortly before demolition. No. 21's entry is this side of the baker's shop.

My two younger brothers and I were born, first door, first flat in stair No. 21, St. Leonard's Hill, which faced towards the bottom end of Beaumont Place. Beneath was Weir's, Newsagent, Confectioner and Tobacconist and to the left of the stair entry a baker's shop. The families lived at the rear of their shops. There were four levels of flats above the shops, with four families on each landing. So with an average of three members per family there were probably close to fifty individuals in each of the stairs in the street. Added together, this massively outstrips the number of those living there today - a good or bad thing? There were two other families on our landing and six on two landings above. So in the tiny space now covered with grass, trees and a variety of weeds there once flourished – lived, breathed, bred and died – some forty or so souls during my stay there and no doubt for many years afterwards.

The grassy area once occupied by 21 St. Leonard's Hill, my birthplace, with Salisbury Crags in the background

But this is only part of the story. Our stair was only one of five or six in that small part of the Hill, extending to Heriot Mount on our side and Carnegie Street on the other, a distance of a mere seventy-five yards or so. In addition there were at least two houses with their main doors on to the pavement. All told, I would estimate that there were about sixty families living in this short stretch. Apart from Weir's and the baker's shop there was a potato store for Macogini's fish-and-chip shop, kindly old Mrs Slater's wee sweetie shop, another selling sugarallie water drinks and, more controversially as far as the police were concerned, skeechan. This was a kind of beer made from brewer's malt and treacle, and intoxicating. Next was a licenced grocer and finally, at the now departed Heriot Mount, a barber's shop.

Crossing the street, we came to No. 10, a ground-floor flat with entrance on the street, Davy Watt's pub, a favourite with my paternal grandfather who lived close by in No. 8, a dairy, No. 16 and finally, at the corner with Beaumont Place, Rutherford's wholesale place. Further afield in Carnegie Street there was Macogini's fish-and-chip shop, a newsagent and tobacconist, a fruiterer and another licenced grocer. There was a little down-the-steps shop selling briquettes for the fire – my main memory of its wares – at the corner of Forbes Street with Beaumont Place. In St. Leonard's Street, just along from Beaumont, were another licenced grocer, Bennett's Engineering Works and Charlie's fish-and-chip shop. Which reminds me of another event which advised us of the time of day. Punctually at one o'clock Bennett's big Clydesdale, having been unhitched from his flat cart, would trundle unescorted towards his stable in Forbes Street for lunch. But first he would stop beside the shop and to the delight of young onlookers like myself would release a stream of hot yellow liquid to flow into the gutters. Its pungent smell is still with me.

At the other end of St. Leonard's Hill, and close to the school, there was another dairy and yet another sweetie shop. Need one go further in trying to describe how vibrant this small area of Edinburgh used to be? So far as I could see, the only survivor of all these establishments was the Jeanie Dean's Pub. An earlier victim was the sweetie shop in Dalrymple Place owned by my maternal grandmother, who had been left it by her mother. This was before and during the Great War, after which the family left the district.

Apart from the shops there were, of course, the coal-men and their horse-drawn lorries; Hugh Leckie with his always attendant Airedales; Mr Brotchie in dark suit and collar-and-tie. I can still picture this stout, red-faced gent leading his horse and calling, "Coal! Shilling a bag! Coal!" as they entered the Hill from Carnegie Street. He carried his money in a leather shoulder-hung satchel. The Clean Air Act of the Seventies and the introduction of North Sea gas for heating and cooking in the home confirmed the end of this era.

The chimney-sweep's was a common cry as the one at the fireplace called out "Swe-e-ep!" to his assistant who had the difficult and dangerous task of identifying the chimney to be swept from the many stacks crowding the tenement roofs. There was a constant "swee-e-ping" from both parties until they were satisfied they'd made proper contact. The wrong choice – and the weighted brush lowered into an unprepared household – could, at the very least, be very messy.

There were too the calls of the chestnut men, the knife-grinders and the ice-cream men as they pushed their specially designed barrows along. And of course there was "Ingan" Johnnie, his bike laden with onions from his native Brittany.

The scaffy was a regular visitor with his wide wooden barrow and a long-shanked besom which he wielded expertly along pavements and gutters. My father told me how potential scaffies were tested before being taken on. They had to sweep a piece of dog turd three times round a lamp-post without breaking it! A more factual story was told by my mother. One morning while I was still an infant she put out the bucket onto the edge of the pavement to be emptied. However, the extra bundle of old newspapers she'd tied together came apart and scattered along the street. She was summoned to court for transgressing a bye-law, told by the sheriff she was a "dirty b-----" and fined five shillings. Needless to say, she was mortified. Would the city benefit from such a tough line today, when main streets – never mind back streets – can be strewn with litter?

I suppose home was fairly typical of those of the majority of the population then. There were two rooms, one a bedroom where I shared a bed with my two younger brothers, the other the kitchen where our parents' bed fitted snugly into a recess. Here too was the sink and wooden bunker beneath the window which looked out over the Flaggy to Salisbury Crags, and a black iron range which, stoked with coal, was the heating, cooking and supplier-of-hot-water. Cleaning out the ashes and burnishing the surfaces with Zebo, brushed in and polished, must have been a tedious daily routine for our mother and countless others like her. Hundred-weight bags of coal were humped upstairs by the coal-man and emptied into a bunker behind a door in the lobby. What a job for these men! Out in all weathers and shouldering bag after bag up flights of dark, narrow, winding stairs.

The only other source of energy was evil-smelling town gas. The house was lit by it, and on each landing there was a gas lamp with its flimsy mantle which as far as I can recall was lit and doused each day by a wee man with a long pole. He used this on the gas street-lamps as well. We had a gas fire in our bedroom and our mother ironed the washing she'd taken from the wash-hoose in Simon Square, and dried on the pulley suspended from the kitchen ceiling, with an iron heated by gas. (A rubber tube connected the iron to an outlet beside the range.) The smell of gas there and in the stair still lingers in my memory.

I will always remember my first day at school – St. Leonard's Hill Primary. Once the parents had gone, Miss Gray, the Headmistress, told us to find seats – girls at the front and boys at the back. I found one in the back row under a window and was very peeved not to be chosen by our teacher, Miss Logray, to pull the ropes to open this window. She chose "the boy with the red cheeks" sitting beside me, Bain by name. This was my first setback in a long, disciplined career. Young Coates of the blond curls fared even worse. In front of the class, in a pool of water, he broke down and cried for his mammy.

So, how did we occupy ourselves when not at school? The wireless was still in its infancy and the only broadcast I had listened to was through the ear-phones of my maternal grandfather's crystal set – and that only snatches of news and weather forecasts while he fiddled around with the cat's whisker. My parents encouraged me to read and once I'd got the hang of it I could hardly wait for the weekly arrival of the Skippers, Rovers and Hotspurs with their cliff-hanging serials. They may have been classified as comics but they were literature compared with their successors, the all-colour, balloon-captioned comics so popular today. Still, I did find The Children's Newspaper, a publication dealing with science and current affairs, a bit heavy at the age of seven: it was my father's idea to buy it for me.

We had our street games too, of course, mostly defined by one's sex and the time of year. There was a time for the laddies to play with whips and peeries (tops), while the lassies had diabolos, hour-glass-shaped wooden objects which looked like two peeries joined together, manipulated on a length of string tied between two hand-held sticks. They would raise and lower each stick so that the diabolo was balanced as it ran up and down the string. The more expert could flick it into the air, catch it on the string again and run it back and fore, ready for the next throw. Meanwhile we chaps with peeries had great fun with windae-brekkers. These were small and shaped differently from the usual peerie – more like a rounded T. Handled properly, they could be launched in an ever-increasing trajectory at some force, for quite a distance. One old lady in the ground-floor flat next to the jannie's at the bottom of Beaumont Place and worried about her windows, used to chase us away with loud screeches. Another time it would be peeverie beds for the lassies and girds for us. These could be old bicycle wheels propelled by a stick, or perhaps car tyres for those strong enough. More sophisticated was the metal-hoop type with cleek but this was only for those whose parents could afford to buy it.

Only the lassies played with skipping ropes, individually or as a group. There could be a dozen or more running into and to and fro over the rope while a lassie at either end ca'ed it. "The wind, the wind, the wind blows high" was only one of the many songs they'd sing in time with the swinging of the rope. I can't remember any more. I didn't want to be called a cissy, which I would have been had I joined in. No, we were more interested in making guiders and hurling on them down the slopes of the Beaumont Street pavement and the steeper one from James Clark's school gates to that end of St. Leonard's Hill opposite the entrance to the coal depot. All that was needed was a wooden box or a few planks, four pram or go-cart wheels with their axles, a length of rope and a few nails, a little bit of applied science and we were off.

There were communal games too. Both sexes would play Kick-the-Can together. Ideal hiding-places for those the one who was het had to find were in the cellars of No. 8 St. Leonard's Hill, below where my father, his four brothers and three sisters were brought up, and in the dark, musty passages beneath the tenements of Beaumont Place. Perhaps the game that sticks in my memory most, because of the hilarity it caused, was cuddy loup – played usually, as I remember, on autumn evenings just as it was turning dark and the street lamps were being lit. The head of the cuddy would stand with his back against the building where Weir's bill-boards were displayed, with the body, consisting of half-a-dozen or more boys and girls with arms around the waist of the one in front, bowed in a line before it. The object was for the other team to loup over the cuddy's back. The first member of the team had to get far enough along to allow for those following, as had the second and third and so on. If the cuddy stood firm under the weight that team was the winner and it became the other team's turn to be cuddy. But if the cuddy collapsed it had to take another turn. Lots of tickling and giggling and hilarious scenes after the collapse of the cuddy – and very few winners.

Bools was another favourite game. A group of us would gather round a hole dug between two setts on the road and thumb-flick the bools into it. These were multi-coloured glessies – or the much larger dollicker. Parents had little to worry them in those days when their children played in the side-streets.

The King's (now Holyrood) Park was a great place for sledging when the snow came – if you had a sledge! I wasn't that fortunate and had to make do with my mother's shovel. Snow came once when we had a Shetland collie called Jackie. I sat on the shovel with its handle pointing forward between my legs, one hand holding it and the other gripping Jackie's leash. It worked quite well until Jackie tired of the game or quickly changed direction. Needless to say, the seat of my rather damp shorts was a subject for a telling-off when I got home. Most boys wore short trousers all year round and only graduated to longs when they started work at fourteen. Very few stayed on at

school beyond that age.
In the Autumn of the same year, 1931, I got home from school to find my mother upset because Jackie had run out of the house when she'd opened the door to a caller. She'd searched the local streets but couldn't find him. The fear was that he had gone into the park, where at that time there were sheep. As a Shetland collie he might harass them. With this in mind I made my way there.
Entering from St. Leonard's Bank, I made my way in the direction of Duddingston Loch, then veered up on to the Radical Road. It was getting dark by then, so with no sight of the dog and finding myself opposite what was then James Clark's School, I decided to make my way from the Road straight down the scree-covered slope rather than retrace my steps. Another occasion when my shorts were badly treated!

A few months later when we were in Niddrie Mains, my brothers and I were walking to Sunday School when we caught up with a man leading a dog the image of Jackie. I remembered seeing this scruffy individual coming out of one of the St. Leonard's Hill tenements some time before and now, like us, he must have moved. When I called out 'Jackie' he seemed to show recognition, but his new owner growled out something and walked on. We never got another dog.

My pals, Dod Mackintosh, George Smith, James Howieson and I spent many hours playing Cops and Robbers or Cowboys and Indians on the Flaggy (some of the bigger girls would cut and sew canvas sugar bags as chaps for us), while some older lads furtively smoked cinnamon sticks behind a dyke. From this vantage point we saw the Graf Zeppelin fly over the city.

A number of annual events kept us occupied too. Although Christmas was a working day for our elders, with holidays only at New Year, we went to parties at the Mission and elsewhere and opened our presents on Christmas morning – not a universal event in Scotland then. The family celebrated New Year at my grandparents' in Broughton Road, in the north part of the city, for as long as I can remember. We always stayed about a week and thoroughly enjoyed the novelty of drinking fruit cordial and eating lots of mandarin oranges: the kind wrapped in silver paper. My father would provide a goose for the New Year's Day dinner which my grandmother roasted in her range oven.

My grandfather, a lithographer to trade, had been a boy soldier in the Seaforth Highlanders and was in the first party of British troops to occupy Cyprus in the 1870s, as a drummer in the pipe band. During our stay he would demonstrate how to hold and use the drum-sticks he gave us along with a hide-covered board, to paradiddle. We got a bit bored with it after a while but always asked for the drum on each visit. His stories of the places he'd been stationed at and the characters he'd been with enthralled us as we shared his bed of a morning. We liked, particularly, his tales of the tailless apes on Gibraltar.

Easter was the time when we would roll our chocolate eggs in their silver paper down the hill in the Park, behind James Clark's school. We weren't too keen, though, on the eggs my mother used to hard-boil and dye. St. Patrick's Day was the occasion for a battle between those declaring themselves Scotch or Irish. Newspapers were packed into a ball and tied around with string, with another long piece of string for holding on to. (If you were a cheat you included a stone in the wrapped paper.) You now had a weapon to hit the opposing nationality with, though there seemed to be fights between streets regardless of nationality or religion.

The same groups did battle at Bonfire time, this time for firewood. We raided each others' collections. Our usual target was a pile stored in an area in Heriot Mount which we could get to easily from the back of our tenement. Our material was used to fuel the bonfire at the junction of Forbes Street and Beaumont Place. Once this was well ablaze our father would take us on a tour of the other bonfires in the neighbourhood. It was a busy night for the Fire Brigade, whose bells sounded in all directions. At the age of four or so, my pals and I would knock on doors in our and other tenements round about Hallowe'en: we weren't too fussy about the actual date. As soon as we heard a door being opened we would burst into: "Please to help the guisers, the guisers, the guisers! Please to help the guisers and we'll sing you a bonnie wee song!". I don't know that we had a bonnie wee song to give them had we been asked - more than likely the harrassed housewife would be in the middle of getting her husband's dinner and would chase us. (I think we got the odd jam piece, though.) Going back to Bonfire time, I remember how we went round the stairs shouting: "Ello! Ello! Bonefire wuid!" in the hope that someone would give us material for the fire.

With events like those and a two-week family holiday at resorts such as Kinghorn or Burntisland or Montrose, the eight years living in St. Leonard's Hill were among my most memorable.

I think this community was typical of the times in many parts of Edinburgh and probably other Scottish cities. Most of the residents, wives excepted since few of them worked outside the home, were employed in the various trades: as railway workers, bus and tram drivers or conductors, hospital staff or shop assistants or factory hands. All but very few had left school for a job at fourteen. Families averaged three or four children per household, living in overcrowded conditions, especially where the sexes were mixed. The lack of a bath and the shortage of hot water had a detrimental effect on hygiene and the constant smell of town gas in the home and the overhanging pall of smoke from coal fires must have been very unhealthy. Still, there were many fewer motor vehicles spewing out lead-polluted fumes and creating other hazards to the environment.

My parents followed the tradition of the 'piece'. This is the custom whereby on the morning of a christening a gift was handed to the first person met on the way to the church. On our way to my younger brother's christening I was given this privilege and gave a box containing biscuits, a cake and a half-crown to the paper boy I met on the stair.

Friday nights were the favourites for weddings and we took advantage of this when we gathered round the back of taxis as they were about to pull out with their wedding-bound occupants. A shower of pennies and ha'pennies would be tossed from their windows and there would be a wild scramble. Some of us would bunce (share) what we had managed to collect and spend it on peas and vinegar in Charlie's fish-and-chip shop in nearby St. Leonard's Street. Charlie must have been a very tolerant individual to have allowed such dirty little tykes to sit at his tables with plates and forks.

Now demolished Mission Hall where we went to the Band of Hope and Sunday School.

In the garden of Pop's Uncle, Willie Dewar, in Kirkcaldy

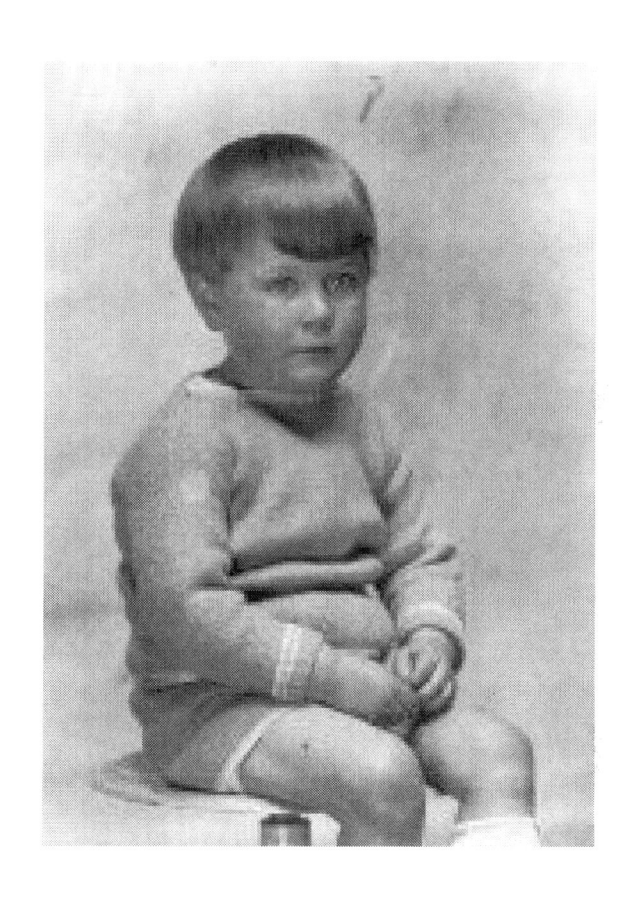

I remember my Father with his camera on a tripod and a black cloth covering his head

David 2, John 4 and self 6 yrs on holiday in Methilhill

The Keelies of St. Leonard's Hill?

Lunch at Duddingston Loch

In the Summer of 1931, St Leonard's Hill School was taken over by James Clark's School as an annexe, thus ending a long family association, for my maternal grandmother had been a pupil there in the 1880s when it was fee-paying. At any rate her mother paid a penny a week to the school for her. After the Easter holidays we went to the school in Preston Street – not nearly as convenient as it meant a walk of ten minutes or so. There was no such thing as school meals so perhaps we carried sandwiches instead of merely crossing the road to the house where our dinner would be waiting for us.

The Primary 2 class with me in the front row 3rd from the left

It was at my new school that I had my first fight, with the class bully, a boy called Pinkerton, who had kept nudging me from behind as we lined up in the playground after break. I turned around and hit him, with the result that he burst into tears. Thus ended his bullying reign - and for the remainder of my short stay at this school I was the class hero. Ironically, 80 years later the same person wrote in a booklet describing the experiences of former pupils of schools in the southside of Edinburgh how he hadn't looked forward to the forthcoming arrival of the keelies from St. Leonard's School – no mention of course of his role at the time.

In 1932 our family left St. Leonard's Hill and made our way to a flat in a building housing only six families, with a bathroom, a separate kitchen with gas cooker, an extra bedroom, electric light, space for a garden, and a strip of trees and a large field behind it. And all of this in the country, only two miles from the city centre.

We were among the first tenants to move into the housing scheme called Niddrie Mains.

NIDDRIE MAINS

Niddrie Mains, which, as the name suggests, had been farmland. There were still wooden bothies across the main road from Harewood Drive, which had housed Irish tattie howkers. I seem to remember some of them still in residence, of my feeling a bit timid and threatened seeing late stayers, scruffily dressed individuals, across the dyke separating them from the bus stop. We were scarcely a mile by road from our old house in the built-up area of St. Leonard's Hill – yet felt we were now in the country, which of course we were at that time, despite the plethora of breweries at nearby Craigmillar, the creamery building next to the bothies and the coalmines not so far distant at the Jewel and Newcraighall villages.

It was only a five-minute walk to the open fields stretching on either side of Craigmillar Castle Brae and down past the castle to Little France. At that time the castle was an unattended ruin and had been a residence of Mary, Queen of Scots. As kids we played freely there without chastisement and only once it was recognised that here was an important part of Scotland's heritage, worth preserving – and the danger to it from vandalism – was it taken over as an ancient monument and policed by uniformed attendants. I doubt whether the Luftwaffe was trying to rob us of this heritage, though, when one of its bombers dropped a stick of five bombs into an adjacent field in 1940. More likely it was Hammon's fireworks factory in the nearby quarry that was its target. Even then, one has doubts about the ability of the navigator to pin-point such a small target, of doubtful strategic value in these early days of the War. Or even afterwards. No, I think the bombs were jettisoned because the crew were lost and wished to conserve fuel. This episode must certainly have caused alarm amongst the members of the Local Defence Force (LDV, later The Home Guard) who were patrolling the area at the time.

So not only was the family taken with the countrified nature of the area but also overwhelmed by the facilities of our new flat. We now had electricity, and gas for the cast-iron cooker supplied by the Town Council. This item was in a separate scullery with large twin tubs for dishes and laundry. There was an actual bathroom with flush toilet, a bath and wash-basin, hot water being obtained from the copper storage tank, heated by the back boiler behind the sitting-room coal fire. Our parents had their own bedroom with an open fireplace, while we three brothers shared a double bed in the second bedroom – without any means of heating. There were no sockets for electric fires in those days. I think it must have been the 1970s or 80s before they became standard fittings in new or renovated council houses, if not most private dwellings. It was so cold at times that we would lie reading in bed wearing gloves. That was one disadvantage, because in the bedroom of our old house there was at least a gas fire. Another disadvantage was having to feed the gas meter with pennies and the electric meter with shillings to maintain the supply. Many was the winter evening when the family sat by candle-light awaiting the return of Pop from his work, hopefully with a shilling in his pocket. It was not that as a family we were particularly hard up but that my father kept my Mother to a very strict budget so that there would be enough money for us to enjoy a fortnight's holiday every year, usually at some boarding-house in Montrose, where we were close to the beach and the golf-course.

Though not well paid at his job in the Royal Infirmary, he had a steady income supplemented by payments from doctors from all corners of the globe in Edinburgh studying for their M.R.C.P. exams. They came to him in the evenings for lectures on the uses of the Cardiology equipment he operated and how to read the electro-cardiograms he developed and printed in the darkroom of his laboratory. He was a pioneer in the field, having been engaged in it since 1920 when taken on by the University of

Edinburgh. So from this humble start as the sole technician, he retired in 1961 with four assistants. I believe the present-day staff now totals 30 persons.

In the 1950s he became a founding member, Chairman and Fellow of the Scottish Cardiology Technicians' Society. However, my most memorable moment was when he came beaming from work waving a £5 note – his wage for the week – a keynote event. This was in 1939, when one could buy a man's ready-made suit for £2 10s at the multiple 50-shilling tailors'. Success at last!

Another asset acquired with our new home was a piece of land behind the back green allocated to us for a garden. This was the centre part of a strip shared by our neighbours, one above and the other on the ground floor. There was a similar arrangement for the other neighbours in the stair, the two lots being separated by a path.

Residents were encouraged to cultivate their gardens and to this end a scheme was formed whereby one could rent a spade, fork (grape), rake etc. for a penny a week by going down to the large hut by the football pitch, a form of community centre. My father took full advantage of this until such time as he purchased his own tools.

As a born and bred townie he had no knowledge, less experience of gardening. Yet within a few years of hard work at weekends and on summer evenings he had a display of flowers and vegetables judged best in the district for three years in succession, for which he was allowed to retain the winning silver cup. Further, he was awarded a certificate of merit by "Home Gardening" at the 1935 Niddrie Flower Show. By this time he'd acquired the two garden areas allotted to our neighbours, who were quite willing to release them. That is, until the start of the

War, when our downstairs neighbours claimed their section back, which of course did seem a bit much after my father's efforts. It was only fair that they were told by the authorities to dig up the strip of grass at the front of their house and grow vegetables there, and be satisfied with that. The other neighbour's plot had not been very fertile, resting as it did on sheets of sandstone, as we discovered when we and they dug down to make way for our Anderson air-raid shelters.

Despite the slight acrimony over the ownership of the garden, which occurred long after our arrival in the building, we and our neighbours had a harmonious relationship, though tinged perhaps with some envy because of our apparently favourable economic circumstances compared with the two families with whom we had most in common. Our family consisted of three boys, and later a girl, where there were three boys in one and two in the other, nearly all of matching ages. Whether the two girls in each of the families were older or younger was of little consequence – they hardly counted at that time, or even later so far as we boys were concerned. Having our mothers chastise us at times was enough without having to put up with the same from the girls.

MY PARENTS

My father, Robert Philp Danskin, was born on March 17th 1896 at Old Assembly Close on the Royal Mile, Edinburgh, and in time grew up with four brothers and three sisters, until through tragedy he was left as the only male member fifty-four years later. William lost his life while with the Royal Flying Corps during the First World War, as did David of the Dragoon Guards. Although James survived this war he was to die of TB soon afterwards, in 1926, as a result of his time in the trenches. And in 1950 Harry, the baby of the family, was killed while inspecting work being undertaken on a building in Drumsheugh Gardens while employed by Edinburgh Corporation. He fell to the ground from a ledge seventy feet up. The father of this large family, my grandfather David Danskin (1864–1943), left his birthplace in Kirkcaldy for Edinburgh where he became employed as a tailor, much to the annoyance and disappointment of his two young sisters, who had urged him to enter the ministry of the Church of Scotland.

Grandfather was an avid reader all his life and had read through the Bible umpteen times. In fact, in later years he would be visited by the minister of Greyfriars Church, when they would discuss the topic planned for the following Sunday's sermon. It does seem likely that his leaving home for Edinburgh was with the intention of applying to enter the ministry, but for some reason or other he wasn't accepted. In any event he ensured that his children were well grounded in the gospel when he insisted upon them attending church three times each Sunday.

Both he and my grandmother, who I remember as a small, spare woman, monosyllabic and lacking the warmth of my maternal grandmother, must have suffered as one by one they learned of the deaths of their offspring. There had also been the news of my father being badly wounded on the Somme . It seems to go without saying that such an accumulation of tragic events must have had a strong bearing on the appearance and outlook of these unfortunate parents as the years passed by. Perhaps it was the cynicism they produced that led to my grandfather turning to the writings of Karl Marx in later years.

At the age of five my father started school in the building on Castle Hill now converted to a Whisky Heritage Centre. He maintained that his teachers during his school years made the mistake of compelling him to write using his right hand when he was, in fact, naturally left-handed. This led to the life-long difficulty he experienced with spelling, he asserted. No matter, it also made him ambidextrous.

On leaving school at fourteen he joined a butcher's shop as an apprentice. He must have learned well, for within a few years he was sent to other branches of the company to cover shop managers' holidays. The shop in Montrose was his favourite and Montrose was to become our holiday destination for many years in the late 1920s and up to the start of WW2.

The first butcher's shop he worked in was in East Richmond Street on the south side of Edinburgh, near the main thoroughfare of Nicholson Street. Because there was no refrigerated storage, it was essential that, come Saturday night, all meat and other perishable products should be disposed of and not left over till Monday. So, to attract customers, my father and his colleagues would stand outside the shop calling out to passers-by and once a crowd had gathered would throw rabbits into it. Those unlucky enough not to get one this way could buy one in the shop for only sixpence (5p). Other products too were reduced for this clearance sale. It being a weekly occurrence, there were always a number of regulars who took advantage of this.

My father turned eighteen on St Patrick's Day, 1914. And when war with Germany was declared on August 4, he presented himself at the local Army Recruitment Office, only to be turned down because at five feet two and a half he was below the minimum height of five feet four. Had he known what lay ahead he wouldn't have been so disappointed. His three older brothers were already serving and, at this time, still alive.

Then, no doubt with an eye to the future, the Army decided to form groups of the undersized but keen volunteers into a separate body and call it The Bantams. Soon my father and his chum Bobby Rennie were on their way to Barry Camp near Broughty Ferry for kitting out and basic training. However, it wasn't very long before they were absorbed into regiments to replace casualties, and so lost their Bantam status.

My father was posted to the 17th Battalion of the Royal Scots, stationed in France. He soon became a corporal; and before going home on leave as sergeant his officer told him to be sure to return with a moustache. No doubt it was felt that a twenty-year-old measuring little over five feet would gain in gravitas with one! A photo of him taken around this time lends weight to the theory.

By this time the family had moved from the Royal Mile to a flat in a tenement on the South Side – 8 St Leonard's Hill, now demolished along with the others in this once vibrant street and replaced with attractive low-level houses. The flat was probably considered up-to-date at the time and appreciated, in spite of there being only three rooms to house such a large family. I have a family group photograph taken in 1912, I calculate, when Grandfather was forty-eight, Grandmother about the same and the others ranging from two to twenty-three years old. So, with marriage and army service accounting for some members, it may not have been so cramped after all, especially after the War ended, of course.

My maternal grandparents and my mother

The Danskin family around 1910

Back row - David, Willie, Robert and James

Front row – Grandmother, Lizzie, Christina, Harry, Grandfather and Peggy

ROBERT PHILP DANSKIN SNR.
17th BATTALION,
ROYAL SCOTS.
1915-1919

My grandparents 1940

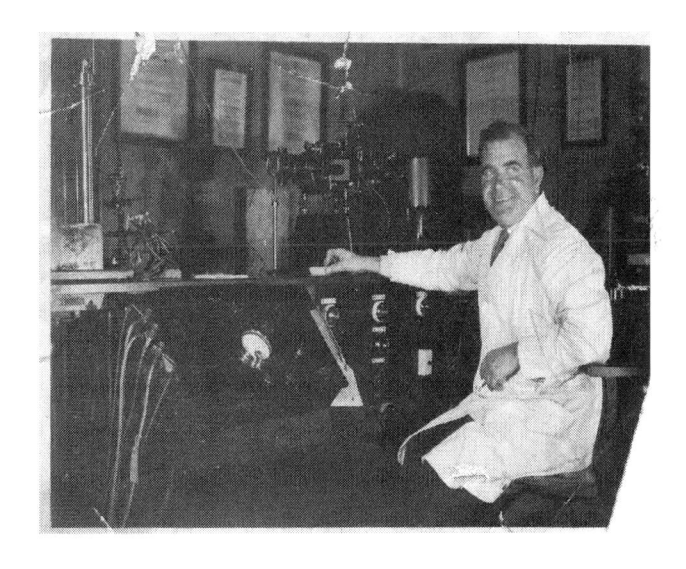

Pop at work in his early days

My parents' 50th Wedding anniversary
1972

Mother and self on day outing to Rothesay

A family holiday in Methilhill in 1929

41

The wedding anniversary get together of the families

I still have a clear picture of the flat in my mind. It was on the first floor, with entrance into a long lobby, with a smallish room to the right where one washed at a small sink fitted into a wooden bunker, the lid of which could be raised to gain access to the coal used in the black iron range alongside, where cooking and water-heating were carried out. There was a table and chairs for meals and another used by Grandfather as a working surface when making suits and other garments for the family once he'd retired. Then there was a rather uncomfortable kist with padding and cushions on top. The window above the sink looked on to the back green and the now built-over Dalrymple Place, a cul-de-sac leading from Carnegie Street, which in those days was much longer, with tenements and shops on both sides. The window provided light during daytime hours and a gas lamp above the fire-place when it got dark.

One of my main memories is the strong smell of tobacco from my Grandfather's pipe, which never seemed to clear from this small space. He smoked "thick black" or something similar. If it's true what doctors say about passive smoking, then this could account for my grandmother's death from cancer of the oesophagus in 1939.

Passing down the lobby, there was a door to the dark WC, then the entrance to the parlour – the posh room with the piano my father bought with the gratuity he received on his discharge from the army in 1919, glass-fronted cupboards full of trinkets, and comfortable armchairs arranged by the gas fire. And, of course, it was nicely carpeted. The window overlooked the street and the uneven numbers of St Leonard's tenements.

The large room at the end of the lobby contained a double bed for my grandparents, a large double wardrobe, black, high-backed chairs stuffed with horse-hair, an agonising seat for a boy wearing short trousers, and a bookcase with bound volumes of Sir Walter Scott, Robert Burns and other such classics – and Das Kapital, no doubt. Leading off this room was a smaller one, Uncle Harry's, big enough for a table, small chest and single bed. It too had a window looking out to the street. Probably there was another gas fire in the bigger room.

My description is of how things were in the flat long after all but my grandparents and Uncle Harry had left. So how were the rooms furnished when most of the family were in residence? We'll never know.

After Grandmother died the flat was vacated and cleared and Grandfather, now in poor health, went to live in the house in St Leonard's Street owned by the now married Harry. He died in

43

1943, aged 79.

As with my grandmother, I never warmed to him. He also seemed distant, somehow. Hardly surprising, one thinks now, with the losses they endured – for not only did they lose three sons, but Christina, their eldest daughter and twin of the dead William, emigrated to New Zealand in 1921. They never saw her again.

I'm sure the experiences of my grandparents were typical of the time, when families were large but decimated prematurely on the war-torn fields of France. One can only guess at the anguish experienced by the parents of servicemen who departed young and enthusiastic and returned severely disabled or not at all.

My father was one of the many who were severely wounded but fortunately not permanently disabled. However, as he got older and into his sixties, the results of his wounds caught up with him.

When he returned to his battalion in France after home leave, equipped with sergeant chevrons and a luxurious black moustache, he became involved in the army's massive preparations for the Somme offensive. I think we're now all familiar with the hardships endured by the troops in the trenches. The mud, the rats, the lice, the constant sound of gunfire. We've seen it all on the screen. But that was only a brief viewing. For troops it was weeks and months in all weathers - rain, snow, freezing cold or boiling sun. All the elements France experiences.

With preparations completed, the moment arrived for the advance on the German troops entrenched behind barbed wire a few hundred yards away. It was just becoming light when my father blew his whistle and led his platoon over the parapet of the trench and on to the shell-pocked ground leading to the enemy. As was the custom, they walked slowly with bayonneted rifles held at the ready. Spread out as they were, and only a few feet apart and upright, they presented ready targets for the machine-gunners, who mowed them down like a machine-harvester threshing corn. And this was where my father got his Blighty.

He suddenly found himself flat on his back following thumps on his thighs. With bullets still whistling overhead, and the knowledge that he'd been hit, he was grateful that he'd fallen a few yards from a shell-hole. While other waves of troops advanced all round him, all intent on their forward movement, he crawled into the crater and hastily looked for the damage to his legs. He must have been bleeding profusely and in great pain. Yet somehow he applied tourniquets or he would have bled to death during the two days and nights he lay there with the battle still going on around him. At the field hospital, the army surgeon, no doubt exhausted, having dealt with very many casualties over the period of the advance, took a look at his wounds and said: "It looks as if your right leg will have to come off."

Fortunately he changed his mind and the wounded sergeant was shipped off to a hospital in Stourbridge, Worcestershire. In later years, suffering with pain in this leg, he was heard to say he wished it had been amputated. He was discharged physically unfit in September 1919, having served three years, eight months with the Royal Scots, two years of that with the British Expeditionary Force (BEF), following a spell of convalescence at the Benedictine Abbey, Fort Augustus; now sadly closed.

In Stourbridge he was adopted by a family called Parrish whose men-folk were in the glass industry. One daughter, nicknamed Gypsy because of her dark complexion, paid him particular attention and even visited our house in St. Leonard's a few years after his marriage. Earlier, the family had sent a wedding present - fine glasses of various sizes with Mother and Father's names inscribed on them.

After such wounds, the deep scars of which he carried to his dying day, and which made one feel squeamish just to look at them, one can only wonder at the energy he displayed during his working life. Walking to work where he was on his feet most of the time. Winning prizes on the bowling-green and for gardening and at the same time playing at least one round of golf a week, weather permitting. Pain forced him to abandon this latter activity as he approached his sixtieth year; though he did soldier on at work until mandatory retirement five years later.

On being discharged from the army, he must have pondered on his future. He had served his apprenticeship as a butcher before joining up but probably the thought of humping carcasses around while his leg was still healing didn't appeal to him. So when it was mentioned that a vacancy existed for a lab assistant at Edinburgh University he applied and got the job. However, though employed by the University, his place of work was a small room in the Royal Infirmary. His job was to operate the Cambridge Instrument Machine for determining the condition of hospital patients. He was in on the ground floor of cardiology and this was to be his occupation for the next forty years.

In 1922 my father and mother, Jessie Wilson Mochrie, were married at the New North Church in Forrest Road, now the home of the Bedlam Theatre, and rented a flat in the tenement, 21 St. Leonard's Hill. It was here that I was born in 1923, and brothers John and David in 1925 and 1927. It was to be another ten years from my birth before our sister Jean was born in 1933, by which time we'd moved to Niddrie Mains. Our mother was fair of hair and complexion, in contrast to my father's dark looks. Both were born in the same year, 1896, she on May 13th in

Milton Street, from where she attended Abbey Hill School.

On leaving she worked as a tea-girl/clerkess with MacLaggan and Cumming, the Warriston Road lithographer/printers where her father was a lithographer. She also modelled clothes for the Art section of the company. Unfortunately, the company boss's young son was so sexually harassing that she left.

When she met our father she was a supervisor with the Singer Sewing Machine Company, with responsibility for sales of machines and parts from the branches throughout the city. By this time she and her parents and brother Johnnie had moved to a top-flat apartment in a Broughton Road tenement, closer to her own and her father's work. As was customary between the wars, she stayed at home to bring up the family and never worked outside again.

Prior to their marriage Pop, as we called him in our later years and as I shall continue to call him here, was accepted in 1921 into the St. Leonard's Freemasons' Lodge and went on to become a founder member of Abbotsford Lodge in Morningside Road. In time he was invited to become Right Worshipful Master of St. Leonard's but felt obliged to refuse the honour because of his financial situation. (At that time in St. Leonard's Hill he had a large framed picture of Rabbie Burns, another Freemason, on the wall of their bed recess.) The position would have incurred financial outlays which he could only have afforded at the expense of the family.

He was probably earning about two pounds ten a week at this time and it wasn't until the early months of WW2 when he came home one Saturday lunch-time flourishing a brand-new note and with a big smile said: "Look! My first fiver!", that he felt he was making progress. The thing was that until 1948, with the introduction of the National Health Service, he was paid by the

University, notoriously bad payers. I believe he did much better under the NHS except when he approached retirement. Because of his having been on the University pay-roll the NHS disclaimed responsibility for the 28 or so years he'd worked in the Infirmary. It took many months of negotiation and arbitration before agreement was reached in his favour. Somewhat similarly he had to fight for a disability pension because on his discharge from the army he'd opted for a lump sum rather than what seemed then to be a miserly pension. Fortunately his claim for a disability pension was eventually recognised and carried forward to our mother on his death. One can but admire his ability to provide so well for his family and for his own pursuits on his lean income during the early years and just before the War. My contribution from a weekly wage of just 11 shillings when I first started work in the Post Office in 1937 could hardly have made much of an impact. What must have had a considerable bearing was Pop's extra money from lecturing.

Over the years doctors from a variety of countries came to Edinburgh for exams which would qualify them as Members of the Royal College of Physicians (MRCP), a much sought-after qualification. Since Cardiology was high on the agenda, candidates would come to my father's lab, two or three evenings a week, where he would lecture them on the routines of his work. With the experience he'd gained over the years working with such distinguished men in Cardiology as Professors Murray-Lyon, Dunlop, Hill and Gilchrist (the last the bane of his working life), he was able to explain much of what could be read into the photographic records, which showed the impulses transmitted from patients' hearts via the machine he operated. He was paid for these lectures.

This must have been the source that enabled him to make sure we enjoyed a two-week holiday – at Montrose, usually, that paid his annual membership fees at Prestonfield Golf Club, assured membership of the Royal Scots Club and that bought tools for the garden, as well as keeping us well-fed and clothed. Pop was very methodical and disciplined with his earnings and kept our mother on a strict budget, but was never mean. A bit self-indulgent perhaps? Well, until the price of cigarettes went up in 1940 he was a heavy smoker. He stopped smoking overnight and never smoked again. He liked a glass of beer and a dram but refrained from this pleasure for the months following our summer holiday until Hogmanay – on the stroke of midnight.

He had the ability to concentrate and try to perfect any task he set himself, sometimes to the point of frustration and chagrin for the onlookers. For example, the minutest attention to detail while painting and decorating or tending the flowers in the garden. He would read up on the subject in hand and consult the experts. He may never have acquired the same expertise himself, but he still managed to win prizes for his efforts. An umbrella at lawn bowls, retention of a silver cup after three consecutive years' wins in a garden competition. A certificate of merit for his flowers, judged by a gardening magazine. He wasn't a spectacular golfer but could still manage to beat his sons – not only by speaking them out of it but also because he was more competent on the approaches to the greens. One of his favourite golfing stories related to a custom at the club whereby four senior members would tee off at the first hole at 9 am on New Year's Day, with the winner of the hole having the doubtful pleasure of buying each member assembled in the clubhouse a DOUBLE whisky. This particular year's winner was a little businessman called Alf, who ordered up SINGLE whiskies. Whereupon the senior member stood up, raised his glass and said: "To Alf, and a Happy New Year until June!"

Pop was forced to give up golf before he retired, his legs giving him too much pain. However, he still visited the club, where he would enjoy a "refreshment", as he put it, while playing dominoes with the others.

He was good at dominoes, just as he was at card games. He had the art of knowing which still remained to be played. I remember him saying how they played cards for money in the trenches in France, so it is most likely he got his training there. He knew a lot of games and we often spent evenings at one or other of them. Most of their names, apart from whist and chase-the-ace, escape me. We had only the wireless then and no TV to distract us.

Buying and setting up our first wireless was a good example of his thoroughness. On the advice of a Mr. Fouldy, an electrical engineer from Heriot-Watt College who serviced the Cambridge Instruments at his lab, a Pye set was purchased. We were now living in Niddrie Mains and had electricity to plug it into, whereas most people at that time had gas only and depended on wet accumulators for their wireless. This was a chore since they had to be recharged periodically at appropriate premises outside.

Mr. Fouldy was present for the installation of our first wireless. On his recommendation it was mounted on pieces of crystal at each corner and the aerial cable trailed through the house and outside to a tree about three hundred feet away.

Until the War years the only programmes I remember are Henry Hall and his orchestra, the News and fat-stock prices, Auntie and Uncle something or other and, most riveting of all, the Test Cricket from Australia, listened to at 4 a.m. From 1939 onwards, though, things brightened up, with ITMA, Arthur Askey, etc. During the War we'd be alerted to a forthcoming air-raid warning when the local transmitters were closed down and only a faint programme sound could be heard from distant transmitters. That was the cue to head for the shelter at the bottom of the garden.

A few weeks before war was declared on Germany on September 3, '39, each household was issued with an Anderson Shelter (named after Sir John Anderson, the Home Office Minister at the time). It was made of heavy corrugated metal, in sections which had to be bolted together to form a rounded structure with a narrow entrance. With our upstairs neighbours Pat and Bob Kane (brothers of Jack, future Lord Provost of Edinburgh) we, Pop, John and I, dug a large hole into which both assembled shelters were sunk. Later we were to cover them with soil, build a sandbag wall at the entrance, steps inside for access and benches along the inside walls. However, before we'd even finished digging the hole, difficult because of the sheets of sandstone just a foot or so down, we heard Neville Chamberlain's radio broadcast. Then within minutes the air-raid warning sounded! Because of the propaganda we half expected fleets of Luftwaffe bombers to come flying overhead but it did seem a bit too soon following the war declaration. And so it proved – it was a false alarm. But not later in March 1941 when the Luftwaffe bombed Clydebank. The family, including my Grandmother, had retired to the shelter after the alarm sounded. Hearing aircraft engines and the sound of anti-aircraft gunfire, I climbed out to have a look and saw a plane looking like a white moth as it was coned by searchlights from both sides of the Forth. Calling the others to come out and look at this spectacle, I hastily shouted for them to go back in again as I heard a 'Whee' from above my head. Not easy for my 18-stone Grandmother. Anyway, I discovered the cause of the alarming sound in daylight later on; it was the nose cone of a shell, which had landed only a few feet from where we had been standing. My invitation to view was not a good idea!!

Methodical as ever, Pop bought sheets of plywood which were placed and held by catches on every window of the house so that shattered glass from a potential bomb-blast would be prevented from entering. They also acted as blackout screens during hours of darkness when no-one dared show a light. They were removed in daylight of course.

Apart from his normal work during the War, he spent a few evenings a week fire-watching at Edinburgh Royal Infirmary. This was to deal with any incendiary bombs dropped on the hospital during a raid. None were, fortunately.

At the peak of his career he had numerous unsolicited offers of employment in a variety of countries, such as Australia and South Africa. How different our lives would have been had he accepted! It was the thought of permanent or semi-permanent exile from his and our mother's parents, I think, which was the main reason why he didn't. After all, travel, until the Sixties and Seventies, was very slow. It took at least six weeks by ship to Australia, for example. But staying at home had its compensations, for he was recognised as one of the leading figures in his field when he became a founding member and chairman of the Association of Cardiology Technicians (Scotland), created as a means of setting standards through examinations for new entrants into the ranks and to gain formal recognition for the role of cardiology technicians within the National Health Service. He visited Guy's Hospital in Greenwich a number of times to liaise with his English counterpart. Following his death, our mother arranged for a memorial book prize for the one achieving the highest marks in the annual exam. It was intended that the interest earned from the £100 deposited by her in a bank account would be used for the purchase of the book, but after a few years' uncertain administration of the scheme by the Glasgow-based secretary and fast-rising inflation, the award was withdrawn.

Having written as much as memory serves me about Pop's life, how was he recognised as a husband, father and by others in his communal life-time? To answer this would be an almost impossible undertaking. But it is, I think, worth a try.

As a man he had of course his faults as do all of us but I feel that his achievements far exceeded these when one considers his background. Brought up in a large family with poor resources; a very elementary formal education; severe war wounds and the accompanying trauma; and a lack of inches in stature. They were overcome to a degree that can only be admired. That he and our mother should stay together for over fifty years is itself testimony that their marriage was harmonious and successful. There were blips of altercation as one would expect but as a witness I can confirm that they were short, with no permanent grudges on either side.

Pop had a trait of self-indulgence, if membership of a golf club, taking us on holiday to a place where there was a nearby golf-course, visiting the nearest pub for a 'refreshment' or over-indulging at New Year came within that category. Until the start of WW2 he'd been a heavy smoker and when his brand was Kensitas he saved the coupons until he had enough to get a slim gold pocket-watch. I was given this watch by Mother when he died.

When first we moved to Niddrie Mains he would go to Miss White's restaurant at Surgeon's Hall for lunch and smoke a cigarette between courses, he was so addicted. Yet, with will-power he stopped smoking overnight and from then, 1939, he never succumbed to the weed again. I think it was a combination of increased prices and the likelihood of scarcity because of the War which decided him.

Also, there would be times when he would be later than usual in arriving home for tea after work. This was when he popped into the Rat Trap, the pub by the Surgeon's Hall bus stop, for a 'quick one'. That could lead to a slight altercation between parents: "Where have you been? Your tea will be spoilt!". Incidentally, that pub no longer exists.

He also liked a flutter, which once led to brother John and me getting second-hand push-bikes from his winnings when we were about ten and twelve years old respectively.

There were various functions he was invited to over time, but because of our mother's reluctance he refused most of them. Her usual excuse was: "I haven't got anything to wear!". But it seems more likely that life at home looking after the family on a permanent basis made her feel socially ill-equipped to mix with mainly professional people and their wives. Still, they must have gone out together in the early years, for I remember John and myself being baby-sat by Uncle Harry a number of times, when he had us enthralled with a story about German warships and the River Weser he read to us on each visit. Also, I can clearly remember giving Grandfather Danskin a hard time one evening as he was seeing us off to bed. I argued with him about the need to wear our semits under our pyjamas. The usual rebellion of a four-year-old who claimed that this was the way his mother did it!

One of Pop's accomplishments I haven't mentioned was his ability to play the violin. How he learned I don't know. Nevertheless he was considered competent enough to play with the St. Cuthbert's Co-op orchestra when it entertained in what was then the La Scala cinema in Nicholson Street, close to Surgeon's Hall. Later he was to encourage me to play by sending me at the age of seven to a lady tutor in Inverleith Place. I enjoyed this once I was able to read the music of the simple tunes Pop and I played as a duet in the house. Unfortunately, after a lesson which proved to be my last one on the violin, the tutor said to Pop that since my timing wasn't very good perhaps it would be better if I changed to the piano – which I did, with almost disastrous consequences. While supposedly practising on the piano in my grandparents' house I inadvertently set my music book on fire. Because of the poor light in the parlour I had asked for the two candles in the two holders fixed to the piano to be lit. Bored with practising, I sat reading a comic on my lap while hitting a few keys now and then to convince them that I was doing what was expected. When they smelled burning they hurried through, to find my music burning fiercely – a sudden draught had wafted a page on to a candle flame. Result – end of music lessons. None of this might have happened had I not been to the optician's the afternoon of my last violin lesson. He had put drops in my eyes, with the result that I couldn't read the music properly as I played alongside the tutor. I followed her playing note by note, a fraction of a second behind. Hence the unfortunate verdict which robbed me of the chance to be another Paganini or Menuhin. Pop played as soloist on occasions and often at our New Year parties. His favourite piece was Bon Accord.

Pop could be a bit of a prankster, too, much of it at the family's expense: such as when he had Mother quite alarmed one Saturday lunch-time when he appeared at the kitchen door announcing that he would like her to meet Dr. So-and-so who was standing behind him. To her relief, for she didn't feel tidy enough for such an occasion, the Dr. revealed himself as John, wearing a new hat.

Another time, while in the lab, he phoned a not-so-friendly ward sister on the portable telephone which linked him by cable to the ward, which was used to communicate with his assistant when a bed-ridden patient was being tested. Posing as a telephone engineer checking the line, Pop had her standing on one leg, transferring the phone from one ear to the other and – I think this is where she twigged – getting her to hold a glass of water in one hand while holding the receiver in the other. From memory, I don't think she was amused.

Of course, these and his many other pranks could be considered childish by the serious-minded, but I feel that it was an attractive part of his character.

As I mentioned earlier, when we moved to Niddrie Mains in 1931 one of the main advantages was the use of a piece of ground behind the house, shared by the six tenants in the stair and divided by a central path. Ours was one piece of the three allocated on one side of it. Neither of our two neighbours above and below had any interest in gardening, so Pop in time fenced and cultivated the whole strip – probably 100 ft by 25. It was near enough virgin land and he spent many hours digging and riddling and manuring before planting flowers and vegetables. He erected a bower at the gate from tree-branches and a tallish fence from the same materials against which he grew sweet-peas. This fence separated the flowers from the vegetable plot. It's quite amazing the trouble he went to to get the best results. He bought loads of horse manure from the Cleansing Dept. which were brought the two miles or so by horse-drawn cart and tipped on to the street outside the stair. We all helped to transfer it through the building and backgreen and into the garden. This was quite a feat. At other times Pop arranged with a brewery to deliver a load of hops which had been processed in the brewing. On top of all this, my brother John and I on occasion pushed a barrow to Prestonfield Golf Course, where sheep grazed at that time, and gathered their droppings, which we called sheep's pirls. Pop would mix these in an oil drum containing water and in time use this water to spray his sweet-peas.

These efforts were fully justified and much admired. He grew roses, dahlias, lobelia, alyssum and other varieties which were a very colourful sight. Meanwhile our table was well served from the vegetable garden with peas, beetroot, cabbage, sybies etc. – all good organic fare. As mentioned previously, it was ironic how our downstairs neighbour claimed his part of the garden so that he could grow vegetables. However the council told him he could dig the little lawn at the front of his flat beside the street and plant his vegetables there. It would have been a real injustice otherwise. Anyway, having won a silver cup for the best garden in the district in a competition organised by the Daily Record, three years running, he was allowed to keep it. He was also given a certificate of merit in 1931 for flowers entered at a local show.

Imagine my surprise when a few years ago while on a holiday to Edinburgh I saw what was left of the Niddrie Mains housing scheme where I had spent so many years – nothing but a large open space with not a house in sight, all of them having been demolished. I suppose this was one way of ridding the city of a district with an awesome reputation.

I have written a record of how Pop was as a husband. So how would his sons and daughter remember him? Speaking only for myself, I can say that he provided well for his family in terms of food, clothing, holidays and encouragement to progress at school and find employment on leaving. He was a good-natured man on the whole with a sense of humour inclined towards coarseness at times – but though slightly vulgar, not degrading. Generally speaking he was extremely good company. Only when he had a drink too many would he argue so forcefully that he'd cause offence. Politically he was a Liberal. And, following the experience with the Communist-led Electrical Trades Union, who tried to recruit him, anti-unions as they existed during their era of power after the War. Looking back at a distance of 40 years since he died, I find myself full of admiration for his accomplishments in all the areas mentioned and find it difficult to compare those of my brothers and myself favourably with them. His passing at the relatively early age of 76 followed a gall-bladder operation, and heart-failure, of all things. He was not in fact ready for this, as with tears he told our mother with his last words.

He was a man loved or well-liked by those close to or acquainted with him and he and our mother deserved a few more years together, even with the constant pain he endured as the result of his war wounds. Perhaps one could say that his being free of pain was the only saving grace. Words in my head on the night I heard of his death: "Thank God I've got rid of the pain in my bloody leg!" would seem to confirm this.

He was a great wee man!

My next school was Niddrie Elementary, an old red-brick building close to where the housing scheme would eventually terminate at Hay Drive. So we had a walk of about three-quarters of a mile to get to school and back twice daily. It would have made sense for us to have made use of the clean pavement of the main Niddrie Mains Road instead of raising the concern and sometimes ire of the workmen busy constructing the many houses, shops and the church as we picked our way around their foundations, piles of bricks and other building materials and often stretches of mud and puddles, during the early stage of the scheme's development. I left Niddrie School in 1934 at he age of 11, after the "Qually".

On top of the Qualifying Exams, our class were, I think, guinea pigs for the Intelligence Tests – e.g. "What is the odd one out of these symbols?". I didn't know then, of course, that seven years later I would be sitting in a building in the city's Hanover Street with a group of others aspiring to be RAF aircrew, busy working on a similar set of tests.

Niddrie School's pupils were drawn mainly from the coal-mining villages of the Jewel and Newcraighall and from Craigmillar, which at that time was the site of something like five different breweries, most of whose employees were housed in tenements, hard by Duddingston Station, on the city's suburban railway line.

My first memory of Niddrie School is of sitting in a crowded classroom learning joined-up writing. There was a little ink-pot, held in a hole in each desk and the ink, a mixture of powder and water, had a distinctive aroma which reminded me of fried bacon. The lady teacher wandered around showing us how to hold our pens – with our forefinger flat along it and not bent upwards like Arthur's Seat, as she put it. Soon afterwards the class was reorganised and I was in a classroom with Mr. Brown as the teacher. A middle-aged man and veteran of the Great War, he was quietly spoken and was very interesting, and because of this had no disciplinary problems. Sadly, he died following a war-related illness while still our teacher. We all attended his burial in the cemetery at Milton Road, Joppa. His successor was Mr. Polson, a tall figure with greying red hair who lacked the quiet humour and patience of Mr. Brown. In consequence he was faced with a more restive class. When he had difficulty with disciplining one of us he would turn to the Assistant Headmaster, Mr. MacDonald, who was to become Head of the new Niddrie Marischal Secondary School. He would quietly enter the classroom and look around until he spotted the reported miscreant. Then, without a word spoken, he would beckon with bent forefinger for that unfortunate to accompany him to his office, where he would receive four of the best from the belt (tawse). I say four, but no doubt the number of times one's hand was struck depended on the nature of the offence. I became one of Mr. Polson's victims when, during a singing lesson – I think it was "Ca' the Yowes" we were practising for Rabbie Burns' Day, someone brayed aloud out of tune and he picked on me as the culprit. As it happened, I was innocent and protested when he tapped me on the head, but despite my denials I doubt that he was convinced. When I told Pop about the incident he challenged Mr. Polson on Sunday at Prestonfield Golf Course where each were members and at times part of a foursome. Soon afterwards he apologised to me in class, convinced or not of my innocence. Actually, there was a family relationship, for Pop's brother James's wife Mary had been a Polson, but how she was related to our teacher I've forgotten. It must have been a trying time for the teacher, being charged as he was with getting us through our Qually (Eleven Plus). That so many of us did and went on to secondary school must have given him satisfaction and was a feather in his cap.

Another teacher some of us were involved with was "Johnny" Walker. A wee chap with glasses, he organised the school sports, football in particular. I played at left half and continued to participate for a while at my next school, Portobello Secondary, although it didn't go in for football, only rugby and cricket.

One Saturday morning in the winter of 1934/35 I played with the Niddrie School team on a pitch now occupied by Scotland's new Parliament building. After the match one of my colleagues suggested we visit his uncle's club where we'd get a cup of tea and a hot pie. It sounded like a great idea on this wet, cold morning following our hefty defeat by the other school's team. The club was in upstairs rooms above shops and the Arcade in the Scotsman buildings on the North Bridge. As we ate our pie I noticed how the people going about their business around us all wore black shirts. They were, of course, members of Oswald Mosely's Fascist Party who sided with Hitler and the Nazis, as I was to learn later. Still, the meat pie was good!

There was an annual prize-giving ceremony at Niddrie School at which the owner of the Wauchope Estate, the widow, Lady Wauchope, presented books to the pupils who had done best in their subject, such as the Burns Essay competition. Her late husband, Lord Andrew Wauchope, had been the heir to a vast coal-mining-industry fortune but despite this joined the army at the age of 19 in 1865. He took part in a number of actions such as the Ashanti War of 1873 and the Sudan campaign of 1898. Red Mick, as his troops called him because of his flaming red hair, led from the front and was popular with them. He was wounded three times. Later he was to lead the Highland Brigade, consisting of the H.L.I, the Black Watch, The Argyll and Sutherland Highlanders and the Seaforths, in the Boer War. They were to suffer many casualties, Red Mick among them, following an ill-judged frontal attack ordered by the general leading the campaign. The Wauchope Estate is now built-over as part of the Niddrie Mains housing scheme and a Celtic Cross to his memory can be seen in Niddrie Mains Road.

Being ineligible to play in Niddrie School's football team any more, I turned to rugby. This was to be short-lived, for after a game at Preston Lodge where I spent eighty minutes running around on a muddy pitch without even touching the ball, I gave up. After all, at eleven years of age, I was only about four foot ten inches in height, if that, so that I was at a decided disadvantage compared with the other players. Being chosen for one of the cricket teams when the season arrived was a different matter, though, for this was a game where I became more involved, both as a batsman and a bowler. The team, the thirds, played against other schools on our own ground, now the site of the new school, or at places such as Myreside or Goldenacre. Also, the boys in the class formed their own teams, Big Leesie providing a team for those who lived in Portobello, while I recruited members from Niddrie Mains boys. Our venues were the football park at the junction of Peffermill Road and Duddingston Road or the public park and golf-course across from our school. We were sustained with bottles of lemonade and bars of chocolate. Not satisfied with this, a few of us, Willie P., brother John etc, would get out of bed early, run around the field behind St. Francis School a few times, then set up the stumps for cricket practice. When we heard and saw the 7.45 train as it departed Duddingston Station for Portobello, we'd dash home, have breakfast and make our way to school two miles away. At first we'd travel by train, fare a ha'penny (1/24 of the current 5p). Later we were to walk each way, while bussing it at lunchtime. How we detested the little ginger-haired bus conductor with his sarcastic comments and bullying tone and how disappointed we were when we discovered he was on duty.

While I coped well while at Niddrie, being one of the top three in the class, my fortune was to change at Portobello. On arrival at the start of the school year, four classes were formed among the first year pupils – A, B, C, D. It seems that the choice for A and B were for pupils who had been in the school's elementary section

– only four from Niddrie were picked. I learned later that I was dropped in favour of a girl, in order to strike a sexual balance. This was to have an effect on my whole future, mainly on the subject of Maths, because the teaching of this subject was abysmal. The teacher, "Papa" Forsyth, a youngish man, had little patience and a quick temper. There were times when he'd have the whole class paraded in front of him, with our hands held palms up to receive the belt. Obviously he was frustrated by the slowness of this C class, but his teaching methods offered little encouragement and did me little good. Anyway, when Mother and Pop became aware of this, she had a meeting with the Headmaster, Dr. Birrell, who said that I should never have been put in the lower class. And so for my third year I found myself in the A class, and as far as Maths was concerned away behind my peers. I never did catch up in Algebra and Geometry. At the time I couldn't envisage practical uses for these – Algebra in particular – and with Geometry did not swot enough at the theorems. The result was that I was not considered good enough to sit the Lower Leaving exams. Had I had "Wee Wattie" as my Maths teacher throughout, it would have made a big difference, for he had a very good reputation as a teacher and a good picker of winners on the race track. He could be very scornful, though, and could ridicule one in front of the class. For instance, he substituted for the French teacher one afternoon but had no intention of teaching us French. Instead he talked about fishing. Calling me out, he told me to demonstrate how to cross a stream. So, picturing stepping stones, I carefully picked my way from one stone to the next until I reached the opposite bank, to what might be described as his hoots of derision which infected my classmates. He in turn crossed over, taking low slow strides as though the water was up to his thighs. It was not to be the last time I misinterpreted the question and thus provided the unaccepted answer. Of course, there are many times when a question can be ambiguous, as when in my case, or during an exam, for instance, one is discouraged from, or forbidden to question the question!

My teachers at Portobello were a varied lot. For French there was Miss Thomson, good at her job, though a bit highly strung and at times just as excitable as a national of the country whose language she taught. A. E. Kennedy was my Geography teacher. He also was pretty good, though one had the impression of his expending much energy without being entirely effective. I saw him many years later while awaiting Ann, who was a supply teacher at Tynecastle School. I passed the open door of his office where he sat at his desk. He was the Headmaster. But for some reason I didn't introduce myself. Our History teacher, Miss Elliot, was a bit of a joke. Short, stout and fiftyish, she couldn't hold the class together and was subjected to much ridicule, especially when she resorted to using the belt on some boys in the class who were close to six feet tall. With one of these before her she would raise the belt to shoulder height. Then, as she brought it down, the boy would take his hand away, while the belt went on and smacked her leg. A variation on this was when the boy removed his hand, strode to the radiator to warm his hands on it, and then returned for his punishment.

There were three Science teachers, Messrs Hawley, Sutherland and Garrigan, who taught us at various stages. The first, Hawley, was a sprightly individual, with thinning, smoothed-down black hair and a neat military-type moustache, who clicked smartly along the corridors on steel-tipped heels. A bit of a health freak, he claimed that his only food on a Sunday was orange juice. By contrast, Garrigan was reputed to be a defrocked priest and was something close to a sadist if the sight of his belt was anything to go by. He had shortened it, then steeped it in some chemical or other, which made it rock hard. I never saw him use the belt and felt that the demonstration he gave of its powers was enough of a deterrent. Meanwhile, Sutherland was a tallish, cadaverous sort of man, probably nearing his sixties. With his grey-black hair, lantern-jawed features, thick glasses, and always wearing black or dark grey, he looked quite a funereal figure. He was patient and instructive, though obviously lacking the flamboyance of the other two.

My favourite was Miss Cope, our English teacher. Tallish and athletic-looking, probably late twenties or early thirties, she had presence. One look from her at someone misbehaving was equal to four strokes of the belt, which she never used. She and our Gym teacher, Mr Bingham, seemed to be an item, judging by the conversations they'd have just outside the classroom door. Strange, perhaps, but Miss Cope reminds me of an ex-English teacher with whom I'm well acquainted who possesses similar characteristics - my wife.

The Headmaster, Dr. Birrell, was very traditionalist and led the Monday morning gathering of the school's pupils in the Main Hall. He was a fine-looking man, tall, with a good head of carefully brushed, snow-white hair – and like Hawley, as I just remembered, sported a healthy tan. Apart from the school song, which started with "Hail, Portobello! We greet you right proudly!" and ended "Onward, forward we must go – Ope et consilio!", I can't remember much about these meetings. Dr Birrell was a Geographer and one of our textbooks on the subject had been written by him.

A visiting teacher or coach was Jimmy Brash, the professional golfer of Prestonfield Golf Club. He visited the school on occasions and gave lessons to those of us who were interested. Tuition took place at the Gym or the nine-hole course across the way. Little did he and I realise that 20 years or so later he would be giving me further lessons, this time at his club.

Other teachers who impinged on me only in my first year were Mr Saunders for Woodwork (I made a pipe-rack for Pop) and the crazy Art teacher, whose name (but not his mannerisms) escapes me. Looking back, I realise he must have been homosexual, for apart from his way of speaking, he'd drape his belt over his head, with one end curling up like a woman's hair, and mince around looking for laughs.

So that is a fair selection of those whose efforts were to prepare me for the world of work.

A topic much to the fore as I write is that of bullying in schools. It is so nasty a practice that many children have been driven to suicide because of it. And it is not just in Scotland or the UK as a whole that it occurs. It appears to be universal. As a wee smout I too was the victim on two occasions at least, the first of which was my encounter with Pinkerton at Preston Street School.

The second time was later, at Niddrie School, when I was victim of Walter Shaw, egged on by his Jewel mining cronies. In class one afternoon I was disturbed by someone behind me kicking my back. It was more of a push than a kick but very annoying just the same. On my grabbing his feet, I think, he challenged me to meet him outside after school. This was grist to the mill for his pals. However, they were to be disappointed, for following a few telling punches from me poor Walter, the dupe, gave in. There were no hard feelings, for on a chance meeting as teenagers when he was apprenticed to D.C. Smith, Painter and Decorator, in Dalkeith Road, we never bothered to recall our bout, and were quite friendly. Our fight was to have unexpected repercussions, though, as explained later.

Meanwhile, there was an everyday occurrence when two of the older boys did battle in the playground during the dinner hour. Dudgeon, a brewer's son, and Carson from the housing scheme (Harewood Drive) were the combatants. I never did learn the reason for this vendetta, not that it mattered to us younger ones, who looked forward to the daily battle. I can't remember how it ended but only that it seemed to be repeated for many days.

It was probably a year later, while I was at Portobello and walking home from school with a few others one afternoon, that we were accosted by a group walking towards us. They were our former classmates at Niddrie School, who'd failed the "Qually" and remained there. One of them, a brewer's son called Runciman, who I learned later had been taking boxing lessons, picked on me. Since he was the stronger and more prepared than I was to do battle, he won the day, leaving me with a beautiful black eye. That was the last I ever saw of him. There were two other times when I was invited to see someone outside, but I've described these incidents in the RAF section of this story.

Sister Jean was miserable as a girl of twelve or so because of daily bullying by two of her classmates as she waited at the bus-stop going home for lunch. So my advice for her was to smack them on the face next time this happened. She did so and thus ended their bullying. Since it is legendary that bullies are cowards, there must be a lesson here which I think is to face up to them.

Come June, '37, I swapped my short trousers for longs, which was quite a highlight in my life. This was the norm in those days. And it was in my new long trousers that I presented myself for interview at the General Post Office, Edinburgh, in my quest for a job as Boy Messenger (Telegraph Boy). This was at the instigation of Pop, who through his contacts with civil servants at the Golf Club was assured that this first step could lead to the sort of comfortable life-style they enjoyed, as I progressed. Of course he was not able to envisage the post-war changes in the Civil Service which were to down-grade it, particularly following the introduction of the Welfare State and a consequent proliferation of civil servant numbers. Nevertheless, despite my being a fraction short of the required minimum height of four foot ten, or was it eleven?, inches – I was accepted. After almost four years of cycling around Edinburgh delivering telegrams, I had shot up to my imposing five feet six and one-half inches.

Ready for work – July,1937

The next four years were happy ones working as a telegraph boy. They weren't all spent in the saddle riding around in all weathers during a variety of shifts. These ranged from 7 am to 3 pm, the unpopular broken shift 11 to 2 and 4 to 7, and the

1.09 pm to 8.57 pm late shift. There were periods spent on indoor duties when office hours prevailed.

I was at the Post Office Stores in Russell Road for a number of months until sent out again to replace the younger boys because of fears for their safety in the blackout. It was whilst here in early October '39 that I was startled by crackling explosions outside the office. Darting outside to see the cause, I saw against a clear blue sky plumes of white smoke, the result of anti-aircraft shells exploding. Suddenly a German bomber appeared, flying low above the roof-tops and heading towards the city. Then a Spitfire shot into view as it chased the bomber, which crashed in a field near North Berwick. A poor painter was caught in the action when struck in the leg by a ricocheting bullet as he stood on a ladder outside a house in Joppa. He must have been one of the earliest war casualties.

As one can imagine with boys aged between fourteen and eighteen, there was quite a diversity of age and maturity. There must have been about one hundred of us covering the shifts at the GPO, while there were others working from the Post Offices in Portobello, Leith, Gorgie, Newhaven and Morningside. Telegrams and cables were an important means of communication in those days and until people had their own telephones, which wasn't to any extent until the late '70s to '90s. Telegrams and cables were received and transmitted by teleprinters, rows of which occupied a large room in the GPO. Next door was another room which received telegrams by phone. Telegrams for businesses in the vicinity of Frederick Street and Hope Street were put into felt containers with hard rubber ends and shunted along underground through pipes the length of Princes Street by air pressure to the post offices there. Discharging these containers was a job undertaken by messengers. We were well regimented by the Head Postman we reported to. At the start of a shift we'd be lined up and inspected to ensure that we'd polished our brass buttons and badges, had shined our boots, belt and pouch, and wore suitably sober ties and shirts – these latter not being supplied.

The boys at the GPO were the responsibility of a supervisor and four Head Postmen who, as ex-servicemen from the not-so-distant War of '14-'18, must have had their own stories to tell – but never did in my experience. I can still see the individual Head Postmen as they stood at the desk behind a grille, recording on a spreadsheet the number of telegrams, the delivery walk (Walk 7 was the Waverley Station and the Scotsman Office building) and the time and number of the boy given them for delivery. My number was T85 but changed to T71 when I returned from the PO Stores at Russell Road. Our time of return was also noted. Where you went was a gamble. We sat on two long benches, each holding about a dozen messengers, and kept moving up as the one nearest the desk departed. Meanwhile the Head Postman selected the telegrams for the next in line according to the time he'd received them. One would moan when the destination was distant and one's shift nearing its end.

If you were lucky you'd get an interesting delivery such as I had when called upon to deliver a gentleman called Fagan to Prime Minister Neville Chamberlain at Holyrood House. This was a service offered by the Post Office for a variety of reasons such as taking a dog for a walk, although I never came upon that one. Anyway, Mr Fagan, a rather scruffy individual with a coarse voice, trudged with me and a few followers from the GPO to the gates of Holyrood House where I presented a Delivery Note to the policeman in attendance, who in turn passed it to another inside the gates. A few minutes later he returned, saying that delivery had been refused. From memory, I don't think the occasion passed very quietly, but my part was done and I returned to the GPO for my next delivery. Obviously times were tense at this time shortly before WW2 and Mr Fagan had some political bone to pick with the PM, but I'm not sure I ever knew what it was. It did incur a lot of shouting on his part, though.

I think it was 1938 when I was given a pouchful of greetings telegrams addressed to Lupino Lane, King's Theatre. (These were in gold envelopes with a nicely printed telegram inside and usually sent to weddings, birthdays or other causes for celebration.) I had just entered the stage door when the man himself arrived, lathered in perspiration having just left the stage, and took the telegrams from me with a "thank you". He was the leading man in "Me and My Girl" and having the show here was the usual trial before being booked into London's West End. Later my father and I went to see it and were very impressed - so much so that he forecast, correctly, that it woud be a big hit when it went to London. With songs like "The Lambeth Walk" and "Me and My Girl" it was bound to be a success.

Another celebrity I delivered telegrams to was Tommy Walker, the star player of the Hearts of Midlothian Football Club. He was in army uniform while attending a switchboard in the Scotsman Building which at that time - 1939 - housed part of Scottish Command.

A pleasant change was when I spent a few days at the Royal Agricultural Show at Ingleston delivering telegrams and cables to farmers and others in the agricultural business from a temporary post office on the site. The rainy weather made it a bit soggy underfoot, though, which was not untypical, I believe, but it was an enjoyable environment to have experienced just the same.

My Father and I visited the Empire Exhibition at Bellahouston, Glasgow in September 1938 and, apart from viewing the interesting and coulourful exhibits there, we had the privilege of witnessing the launch of the liner, the Queen Elizabeth. There was a massive displacement of water, which raced across the adjoining fields, much to the concern of a large hare, which made a hurried exit. We were not to know that a year or so later the vessel would become a troopship, although there was an indication of the coming of a second World War when the Daily Express stand at the exhibition announced on a moving billboard : "Territorial units are being called up".

The Head Postmen were a mixed bunch. There was Jock Mackay, a big, moon-faced man with a bald head; Jerry Falconer of stocky build, with black, wavy hair; Harrison, a thinnish, greyed individual with lined features; Paul, a small, mouse-like creature whose boy-messenger son had a lung removed and was given the title: Boy Messenger of the Year – a sympathetic gesture which, I was told, deprived me of the honour; and Walpole, a heavily-built blond who was a keen swimmer and instructed us at Infirmary Street Baths. All were probably in their fifties.

The job of Best Messenger was to stand at the North Bridge entrance to the GPO next to the Head Postmaster's office and, along with a Head Postman, receive and direct visitors as they arrived to do business. So this light job was, of course, ideal for young Paul and his physical condition.

Only a few of my fellow messengers stand out in my memory. Some of them were killed during the War. There was quiet, tall, unassuming and fair-haired George Mackenzie, a few years older than myself, who ditched in the Channel in his Spitfire and died of exposure. Full of life Freddy Ball, who worked with me at Russell Road and lost his life as an RAF WOp/AG. Luckier was Jim Monaghan, who had been with us at the Post Office Stores, who left the Navy and became a Church of Scotland minister. We met up in Hong Kong in the Fifties, where he was chaplain to the Forces stationed in the New Territories. Coincidentally, John

Pollock, who'd been Boy Messenger of the Year in his time, was, like myself, a civil servant at the HK Dockyard during the same period.

A former messenger who became a near legend in the Highlands and Islands was the late Duncan MacIntosh. He'd flown Spitfires from Malta and when I spoke to him after the War he was a Flight-Lieut. and CO of the Edinburgh University Air Squadron. It was as the pilot of an Air Ambulance that he became so well known in the Highlands and Islands.

Then there was 'Prof.' Sinclair, over six feet tall, slim and with glasses. He and I went as delegates of the indoor branch of the Union of Postal Workers to an STUC conference in Falkirk in '49 or '50. It was held in the Co-op Hall, where we just about had lunch in the restaurant attached before the proceedings commenced. We were served up a duckling each – or were they rubber balls? - for we were unable to penetrate them with either knife or fork. So we didn't have lunch! I was to replace the Prof., who'd had much difficulty with the Cash Account job, burning the midnight oil at times in an effort to balance the books. By contrast, I would be finished and on my way home about 45 minutes before my time.

John MacGrath was another chap I knew well, especially in the late '40s, early '50s, when we'd go to see the Hibs or Hearts on Saturday afternoon, then meet up later at Milne's Bar for a couple of pints and a chat with his uncle, an ardent Communist. We saw the poet, Hugh MacDiarmid, there at least once.

Another favourite pub was Miss Scott's, the last one at the west end of Rose Street. She was quite a formidable lady who stood no nonsense or unruly behaviour from the many students who frequented the place. In her late fifties, I would say, she was slim, grey-haired and always wore a black suit. I don't know when the pub changed hands but when one evening in the '90s I thought I'd look in for old times' sake, there was a bouncer at the door – and that was enough to put me off.

Chucky Liddell, another messenger, was ineligible for service in the Forces because of deformed fingers on one hand. He was an Assistant Scoutmaster and on one of my leaves I went camping with his troop at a mining village in Northumberland. The local scoutmaster was a miner and invited us to go down the mine where he worked. It was quite an experience, especially when a couple of us entered a two-foot or so high space to reach a cavern where two miners were working knee-deep in water. Above was the North Sea. What a way to earn a living!

The Telegraph Boys' role was to change dramatically in the ensuing years. First, just after the War's end, they were to become Junior Postmen, wearing postmen's uniform. They then gave up their push-bikes for motorcycles. Finally, with the withdrawal of the Telegram Service in the '90s, the delivery of these urgent items and consequently the jobs of those delivering them, came to an end. The profusion of telephones throughout the country and e-mail was the reason for this of course.

On reaching the age of 18, I was to change my uniform for that of postman, another job I enjoyed for the nine months before entering the RAF. I liked the variety offered by this new job, though secure in the knowledge that it would be brief. I learned to drive within a month or two, my instructor being a Head Postman who took me and two others out in a PO van. My first solo took place one evening with a bunch of telegrams destined for addresses in Leith – not a district I was familiar with, since it was normally the messengers from Leith PO who delivered here. But because of the blackout their day finished earlier.

As luck would have it, I drove into a street which turned out to be a cul-de-sac, strewn with firemen's hoses. A Civil Defence exercise was taking place. My lack of experience in reversing caused me some embarrassment when I stalled and had to descend sheepishly and wind up the engine with the starting-handle, in full view of the firemen and CD people. My confidence was dented a little.

In time, however, I became quite accomplished and was soon ferrying postmen to their walks in the Liberton Brae area before going on to do my own deliveries further afield, towards Gilmerton. Most of my driving took place from Strathearn Road and I enjoyed a good rapport with the staff here, though most of them were much older. My one grouse was that though I was doing the same job I only got £2.10s a week as opposed to their £4-£5.

I had only a couple of driving incidents during this period. One was when, in half light, I misjudged the width of a track and went over a bank and into a field of cabbages. Fortunately the van stayed upright – though I found myself down by the pedals. Obviously, having come into and exited the field, I'd disturbed a few cabbages so I returned to the farmhouse I'd left shortly before and reported the incident. As it happened, the farmer was away and the chap who came to the door came with me to the field and helped to right the stricken cabbages, and that was that. Another time was on a wet, dark night as I made to cross the traffic lights at St. Mary's Street, when suddenly a dark figure crossed my path. There was a small collision and the man fell. Fortunately, my approach was just about crawling speed. However, although he got up and walked away, apparently unhurt, I reported the incident to the police station in the High Street. "Forget it!" I was told. It seems that policemen were in a car sitting at the lights the man had crossed from, so he was out of order and seemed to have had a few too many besides.

One of the jobs I did earlier was to relieve the two postmen who operated out of Telephone House on Queen Street when they went on holiday. Their task was to collect the coins deposited in the public phone boxes dotted throughout the city. One opened the drawer holding the money with a special key, then gathered a variety of pennies, sixpences and shillings into a bag. The next thing was to count and roll in paper each denomination to the equivalent value of £1. This was quite a tricky operation, given the small shelf to work on and in such a confined space. The rolls were then put in the Gladstone Bag carried on one's shoulder. As soon as possible the burden was removed by going to the nearest bank and exchanging the coins for notes. Much walking was involved and at times with a very heavy bag. Still, this chore only lasted for a few weeks and helped to build up my fitness for my forthcoming employment with the RAF.

RAF SERVICE

It was on February 25, 1941, the day after my 18th birthday, that I presented myself at the Assembly Rooms, George Street, Edinburgh, as a volunteer for the RAF. Still in my telegraph boy's uniform, I must have contrasted somewhat amusingly to any onlooker with the burly uniformed policeman who joined me at a desk where we filled in our application forms. A few weeks later I was told to report for General Duties. Meanwhile I was enjoying my new job as a postman driver and wrote back asking for a deferment of three months, which was granted. (I didn't learn until sometime later that General Duties was the RAF term for Pilot, else I'd have reported immediately – such is fate.)

In due course I once again sat an Intelligence Test and had a Medical, the results of which would determine my suitability for pilot training. To my delight, I passed again and was told that I could start training for any air-crew job, Pilot, Navigator, Wireless Operator/Air Gunner (WOp/AG), Bomb-aimer or Gunner. However, my heart sank when, after I'd surrendered the form to a corporal, he returned it, amended to read that I was not quite suitable for pilot training – my legs were too short. Had they shrunk since the previous medical which I'd passed? So I opted for Wireless Operator/Air Gunner (Wop/AG). There were a dozen or so others with me at the time and I wasn't the only one turned down for the same reason. The likeliest explanation for these decisions seemed to be that they had a particular quota to fill in each category. For in the years ahead I was to fly with pilots even shorter than myself. Still, I might have failed the pilot's course anyway and, after many hours in the air in my second-choice role, I am still around to write this account.

On December 5, 1941, I made my first sojourn across the Border into England, arriving at Warrington Railway Station early on a dark, chilly morning after the overnight train journey from Edinburgh Waverley. About a hundred of us stood, cold, hungry, waiting for the arrival of the authorities to take us under their wing. Meantime, another train stood at the opposite platform blowing off steam so noisily that conversation was impossible. Added to this was the constant droning of aero engines on test at a nearby factory. So altogether the spirits of this group of potential airmen were rather low as what seemed like hours passed. Suddenly we came to life as an RAF sergeant and corporal arrived, shouting orders to board the lorries lined up outside the station. In no time there was a mad scramble as we headed for an unknown future, still in civvies and clutching small cases or bags from the old world we'd just left.

Our new future was clear enough, however, for no sooner had we left the lorries and reported to the guardhouse than a corporal rounded us up and barked an order for us to pick up any bits of paper etc. lying about the yard. Our first taste of discipline, RAF Padgate style.

Bewilderment followed for those of us unaccustomed to sharing a hut with twenty or so others from all over the UK, with their varied accents and coming from diverse occupations. But at that early stage we were eager to get into uniform and rid ourselves of the rawness we felt in the mess hall in civvies alongside the uniformed veterans of a week or more. Some were betwixt and between as they waited for some item such as trousers, being adjusted by the tailors. After a few weeks of bedding-in as new aircraftmen second-class (AC2), a group of us was sent to the wireless school at Blackpool and an intensive course of square-bashing.

To assess our adaptability with the Morse Code, we attended classes above Burton's the Tailor. It was here they decided if you were to train as a wireless operator. If after four weeks you couldn't cope with receiving at four words per minute, and then up to twelve, you were discarded and had to apply for another trade. It was said that some former coastguards accustomed to sending and receiving at the much faster rates of thirty words per minute found difficulty with the slow speeds and were failed. The contrast in speeds is significant, for 4 WPM, i.e. twenty alphabetical letters represented by twenty Morse symbols sent per minute, is one symbol every three seconds, compared with 0.4 seconds per symbol at the much faster speed.

On being accepted for further training the budding Wireless Ops attended sessions to build up speed in both sending and receiving, at the Winter Gardens.

Although this wireless training was the essential aim of our stay in Blackpool, there were, of course, the military aspects associated with discipline to be learned. First there was the RAF salute, different from the Army and Navy salute, not to mention the Wolf Cubs' and Boy Scouts', which had to be unlearned. A few hundred airmen were gathered on the Empress Ballroom dance floor while an unpopular Sergeant Suttie demonstrated the salute from the stage and had us repeat it over and over again until he was reasonably satisfied with our prowess. A bit of a bully, this sergeant had a reputation for charging airmen for the most minor of misdemeanours. Later that year he was posted to South Kensington, where courses on wireless air maintenance were taught in the Science Museum. Prior to my arrival there, Scots Guards had been called out to deal with a disturbance caused by rebelling airmen in the Albert Court Mansion behind the Albert Hall where they were billeted. It was all over by the time I entered the same billet so the reasons given for such drastic actions were anecdotal. But I believe the burning of bedding and the destruction of various items of furniture had alarmed the authorities. It seemed that Londoners among the airmen were the main culprits, objecting to the order that all airmen had to be back in their billets by, I think, 22.00 hours. This restriction was imposed because of the increasing numbers returning from their evening visits to their London homes just in time, or late, for classes the following day. As part of the rebels' protest they drew, on walls and wherever there was a suitable surface throughout the city, a circle with spokes from the centre to the perimeter and the words "Flywheel says 23.59" underneath. This was the compromise demand.

I left before the problem was resolved, but not before learning of the fate of Sergeant Suttie who, it is most likely, had been sent down from Blackpool to enforce a measure of the discipline he was noted for. One dark evening the sergeant was gathered up by a group with a grudge and tossed bodily into an Emergency Water Supply tank, one of the many dotted throughout the streets for firefighting during air-raids. His ardour severely dampened, I think he must have been transferred, for I didn't see or hear of him again.

Getting back to Blackpool, there are other events which spring to mind, such as the private homes we were billeted in and their avaricious owners. We were shunted around into five different places during our time there. Although it was mid-winter, none of the rooms we occupied was heated. One had a leaky roof. The meals served were skimpy to say the least. For example, at one establishment housing at least a dozen airmen the family could be seen tucking into meat and potatoes etc., having served us with a mixture of black peas and potatoes. And to think how the owner got 30 shillings per head each week – which was quite a fair sum then. In another, lights were switched off at the mains at 10 pm and not restored until 7.00 am. Yes, we were hungry while dependent on these landlords and landladies for our sustenance, so much so that when one evening in desperation we searched our various pockets hoping to find something to buy chips with, we were ecstatic when one of us found a three-penny piece. I should mention that when I say "we" throughout the foregoing and afterwards, it is generally a reference to the four Edinburgh types who stayed together for the first 14 months or so of our service. There was Johnnie from Hill Square, Alec from the High Street, Dod from Portobello, who had been in my year at Portobello School four years before, and myself from Niddrie Mains, of course.

Dod and I first came into close contact during a gym display we took part in at a school concert in Portobello Town Hall. It was arranged that in approaching the buck I should stumble and fall onto it while those behind would leap over me plus buck. This worked well until Dod misjudged his approach and landed on my head – much to the amusement of the audience. I don't think this was a deliberate action by Dod. But I got my revenge, though not intentionally, during a session of unarmed combat in Stanley Park where we had rifle-shooting practice at the butts. The idea was for Dod to lunge at me with a rifle, whereupon I would grab the barrel with my left hand, the stock with my right, and twist my body to the left. We were both surprised, and Dod somewhat annoyed, when he came over my shoulder and landed flat on his back on the muddy ground. Touché!

Another incident of lasting memory occurred while on guard duty at the Imperial Hotel, Blackpool. Our corporal had been keen to instruct those of us involved of the need to be alert and vigilant when posted at the entrance, armed with rifle and bayonet attached. Should anyone approach, he or she should immediately be challenged with a "Who goes there?" and at the same time be presented with a menacing bayonet. I was the sentry around midnight in pitch darkness when I heard hasty footsteps approaching my post. Immediately I made the challenge as instructed, whereupon the figure who loomed up in front of me slithered to an abrupt halt and landed on his behind – it was the corporal! I think he said "Very good!"

George Welsh

Self

*Alec Reid -
killed in action*

Johnny Christie

1942. Dod Welsh and self in Pop's Garden. Just finished wireless course at Compton Basset.

With a basic knowledge of wireless and Morse Code – and our square-bashing - behind us, we headed home for a week's leave before entraining to the Wireless School at Compton Basset, near Calne in Wiltshire – the place where Palethorpe sausages were made.

(I had another go at pilot training while at Blackpool. Airmen were invited to apply to remuster and to present themselves to a panel of senior officers. I attended such a board, and with just a few weeks as an Airman, Class II behind me, I was a bit overawed. However, I did well at answering questions, particularly at being able to point out capital cities on a world atlas, but was finally stumped when given a simple algebra equation to solve. I was told to attend evening classes on the subject before re-applying, which I never did.)

It was a new experience arriving at this RAF station out in the soft Wiltshire countryside. We arrived in early March, 1942, just as the weather was warming up – a pleasant contrast to the winter of Padgate and Blackpool. I can always remember our first Sunday there when we strolled down to Calne in bright sunshine to see what it had to offer. Unfortunately, such shops and cafés as there were were closed. Other places, such as Melksham and Malborough, were out of bounds to us for some reason, so most of our time was spent in the NAAFI or in the camp cinema, or just walking in the countryside.

Apart from the NAAFI tea (a cup of tea and a shaving brush, please!), cider was the only beverage. This I steered clear of, just as I avoided all alcoholic drinks and cigarettes for another couple of years or so, i.e. until my twenty-first birthday, when I succumbed to the social pressures of the Sergeant's Mess.

As expected, our working days were spent at lectures and Morse practice until, after three months, we were considered sufficiently competent to wear the "sparks" badge on the arm of our tunic. We were now Wireless Operators and, to distinguish us as potential air crew, we also wore a white flash at the front of our caps.

A number of notable events occurred at this time, one being the first thousand-bomber raid on Germany. Another was the Baedeker raid by the Luftwaffe on Bath. The glare from the resulting fires was clearly visible to us, as were the sounds of exploding bombs. I'm sure that both events made us all the more eager to finish our training and get into action. However, there was still some way to go before that stage would be reached.

Our first posting as Wireless Ops, still as a foursome, was to an operational training unit (OTU) for Hurricane pilots at Annan in Dumfriesshire. Here we worked in shifts covering 24 hours each day of the week, receiving coded messages, mainly weather reports, which we passed to a WAAF officer for decoding. This gave us a lot of Morse practice, of course. Two WAAF operators shared the duties with us, one of whom, I learned some twenty-three years later, was the daughter of a foreman in the flour-loft of Macvitie and Price at Robertson Avenue I met when working there. She was now married and living in Port William, while her colleague had died shortly after our departure to our next posting. This was sad. I still remember the fun we had cooking up some sorts of meals on a small electric burner during the night-shifts. Cheese, I think, was the main ingredient.

After six weeks we were transferred to another Hurricane OTU, this time at Tealing outside Dundee, where the duties were the same. However, being close to a city, we were not so isolated as previously. It was here that we saw *Gone with the Wind* in a cinema close to the Overgate. It is amazing how changed Dundee has become, for when I visited it about fifty years later my visual memory was completely confused. The couthieness of the centre seemed to have been lost and with various demolitions and modern replacements, altogether it seemed a different place.

An amusing incident I can recall took place at one of those OTUs – but I can't remember which. It was when a covered-in army lorry pulled up on the road outside the camp perimeter and some Italian prisoners of war jumped down from the rear. Then a rifle, followed by a khaki-clad arm, appeared and passed the gun to a waiting POW, whose colleagues assisted their British soldier-escort down beside them Could such an act of trust have been made had the POWs been German, I wondered.

We left Tealing in November, 1942, for an Air Maintenance Course in London which was to last for fourteen hectic weeks.

On our arrival in London we were billeted in one of many rooms in a building situated immediately behind the Albert Hall. Much of the goings-on at this place I described earlier. The guards would be called out to quell a riot, a suicide, arson and I don't know what else. Disgruntled Londoners were the main cause of these incidents, I believe. More amusing was when the mass of airmen attending lectures in the Science Museum retaliated against the corporals who had been putting on a charge individuals caught running along the landings, by stepping slowly step by step up the stairs to the first landing and singing in slow, slow time: "Gone are the days when my head is bending low. I hear the gentle voices calling, "Poor old Joe!". This didn't help the cause of those who wanted to stay out till a minute before midnight.

The course was intensive, with lectures on wireless theory and practical wireless applications and, of course, much sending and receiving of Morse. The lecturers were civilians.

Being stationed in London had its advantages, despite the odd air-raid warning. However, this winter of 1942-3 was relatively free of attention by the Luftwaffe. Nevertheless, people still slept on the platforms of the Underground, as I witnessed a number of times on my return from a night out. Usually a visit to Kensal Rise, where my Aunt Peggy and Uncle Andrew lived with young daughter Elizabeth. This was their second house in the same district, their first having been bombed – when they were outside, fortunately. The space where it had been looked like a gap in a row of teeth.

When the weather was wet, we, our squad, would be taken into the Albert Hall for PT. Not on the main floor, but on one of the balconies, with our footwear discarded. However, most of the exercises, plus a lot of running, took place in Hyde Park, behind the Albert Memorial. Better still, we played an unorthodox style of rugby cum football here with no holds barred, nor gender discrimination, there being a mixture of WAAFs and Airmen in the teams. Should you see one of these going about with an arm or leg in plaster you could almost be sure that he or she was a victim of this vicious game. It was good fun, though.

It was while here that I visited Uncle Jimmy Barclay at India House in Aldwych. He was in fact one of my maternal grandmother's brothers. Previously a regular soldier who had served as a regimental sergeant-major with the Royal Horse Artillery in India, then France, before and during the First World War – and later at Piershill Barracks, Edinburgh and at Hounslow in London, where he retired from the Army in the late '20s and became employed as an indoor messenger in India House in the Strand. He introduced me to one of his bosses, a typical higher civil servant type of that time, a neat gentleman with tidy grey hair and a clipped little grey moustache. Sir Something Kerr, I seem to remember. Very well-spoken, until he revealed his origins by breaking into a strong Glaswegian for my benefit. Jimmy took Dod and me to the Stoll Theatre for a treat one afternoon. But unfortunately the show, a sort of revue, was a dud.

So after fourteen varied weeks in London, with practical and theoretical wireless well under our belts, we left for our next posting. And this was where our long association broke up, Johnny and I going to No. 4 Radio School near Hereford, our first flying experience, while Alec and Dod went elsewhere and I never saw either of them again. Sadly, Alec was killed on ops, though I never learned the details. Johnny was called to attend his military funeral in Edinburgh, just as I had been for the funeral of Dougie Craigie, a Niddrie Mains chum and also a WOp/AG, whose Boston Light Bomber exploded on landing – a bomb hang-up. But Dod Welsh? I just have no idea what became of him.

Poor Alec, slim and fair of hair and complexion, had a cheeky grin which drew the attention of the SP (RAF Service Police), who would stop him in the street for a button undone or other minor reason. I remember the panic when he sat on the escalator steps of the Underground one night, right down to where it disappeared, along with the tails of his greatcoat. I can't recall how he managed to free himself but can picture one ruined garment.

So we arrived at our new station in February, '43, on the 23rd, the day before my 20th birthday, when I flew for the first time. What an uncomfortable trip that was. The airfield was somewhere near the town of Hereford.

Apart from the pilot there were six of us trainees and the corporal instructor aboard the twin-engined Dominie biplane, the kind used to carry passengers around the Highlands and Islands at another time – as depicted by the statue of the man credited with pioneering this service, which stands exposed to all weathers at Dalcross Airport, Inverness.

Anyway, we took off and up in the plane, reaching the desired height. The corporal beckoned to me to sit at the desk above which the transmitter and receiver were fixed and proceeded to show me how to tune the latter. Suddenly he reached down, grabbing the drawer beneath the desk and thrusting it at one of my colleagues, who promptly spewed into it. This was enough to get the others going as the drawer passed from hand to hand to the back of the aircraft. I felt squeamish myself, what with the wallowing movement, the pear-like smell of the dope painted onto the plane's fabric to preserve it, and of course the odour from the contents of the drawer. That I was busy at the desk meant that I was less affected by these things and I was able to rise above it.

We landed one hour and forty minutes later, much to the relief of all, I suppose. But we were airborne again after a respite of only twenty minutes for a different exercise in the use of the Direction-Finding Loop, which lasted one hour. There was no need for the drawer this time.

We all wore a parachute harness over our uniforms which had two metal clips on to which the 'chute was attached should the need arise to bale out. Meanwhile the parachutes, folded within their covers, lay piled up by the door of the aircraft. Once we landed I obligingly handed down the 'chutes to my colleagues, since I was the last about to leave. Unfortunately I grabbed the wrong handle of the last one and found myself enmeshed in a cloud of silk. The nice silver handle I had chosen happened to be the one you pulled when falling freely in mid-air. So amid many chortles I bundled up the mass of slippery material as best I could and trundled to the parachute section. Here I was welcomed with more hilarity by two WAAF packers who promptly demanded a half-crown (12p), the usual penalty for such carelessness. I suppose that in those days that would have been enough for two packs of cigarettes.

In the days and weeks ahead we were to continue with various exercises in the Dominie, such as using the Q Code, tuning transmitter to receiver and direction-finding, then switched to the single-engine Proctor monoplane. Here the wireless operator sat next to the pilot and operated the equipment mounted on a surface to his left, which was awkward, especially when reeling out or in the hand-wound trailing aerial. My flying log-book records a total of 21.45 daylight hours on these aircraft, the last on April 16, 1943. So we were well on our way to qualifying for our sergeant's stripes and air-gunner brevet. However, we had first of all to complete a Wireless Operator Emergency Gunnery course at Manby, Lincolnshire, which lasted for only two weeks. Here we had intensive lectures covering the handling of the guns, Browning .303 and .50, and the use of the radial gun-sight. One sat in Boulton Paul or Frazer Nash turrets and fired at a dummy plane moving at speed around a circular track, which was good fun. This was on the ground, of course. Later we were taken up in an Anson, maybe a half dozen of us, to fire coloured-tipped bullets at a drogue being drawn by a Proctor. Urged on by the pilot with many epithets to hurry and fire while searching around unsuccessfully for a sight of the evasive drogue, I pressed the trigger. For all I knew I could have hit the towing aircraft. We looked at the drogue once it had been released to the ground for evidence of hits, based on one's bullet colours. A waste of time on my part, of course.

End of Gunnery Course Manby 1943
With self second left in second row and
Johnny Christy third from left front row.

It seems obvious that this abbreviated gunnery course was to justify the wearing of the AG brevet and that it was not intended at that stage for us to go to an Operational Training Unit prior to joining an Operational Squadron. This was confirmed by our next posting. This was to 10(o) AFU Dumfries, where we started flying on May 18, 1943 – I as Second W/Op to a Staff W/Op on Ansons, along with a staff pilot, pupil navigator, pupil bomb aimer. Johnny and I had gained sufficient experience for us to be chosen for the Staff/W/Op role at 1(o) AFU Wigtown a few weeks later.

During the three weeks at Dumfries, I spent 18½ hours day and 9½ night in the air on exercises averaging three hours' duration to various points around the south of Scotland, Northern England, the Isle of Man, and Northern Ireland. We attended lectures as well. So if my memories of this posting are few as far as the social side is concerned, it must be because there were few or none of any significance. At least I was back in Scotland and was to remain so for the next fourteen months.

I went home to Edinburgh on two weeks' leave from Dumfries, arriving for the first time with Sergeant's stripes, AG brevet and Sparks badge – a fully-fledged aircrew member! Sister Jean was impressed, as an eleven-year-old would be, of course. I can't remember Pop and Mither's reaction, but I feel sure they were mixed, because of the potential dangers.

The Wigtown airfield I returned to after my leave was located across the road from Kirkinner Railway Station, the terminus of a branch line from Newton Stewart. So one could say that it was practically in the middle of nowhere, so that the hundreds of RAF and WAAF personnel stationed in the camp had to make their own entertainment or rely on that occasionally supplied by ENSA. In summer it had the advantage of being surrounded by lush countryside, and not far from the Irish Sea, with Port

William, an attractive coastal village, an easy cyclerun away. In such an establishment there was much room for drama, for sad times and happy times. But as time went by I became bored and anxious to go on ops instead of dodging around the Minch, N. Ireland, the Isle of Man, etc. There were moments of danger which raised one's adrenalin somewhat, but flying in the middle of the night in an unheated aircraft in winter was decidedly uncomfortable and not very interesting.

On the contrary, though, I enjoyed the sight while flying in clear skies, during daylight, of the Outer Isles, with the variations of blue/green waters surrounding them. Again, flying in the same direction at the height of summer was quite phenomenal. Because of double summer time a midnight take-off would be in daylight. We'd then fly into darkness, into more light at the turning-point, back into the dark, and land in daylight. All this within a trip of three hours or so.

For all the flying carried out here, I can remember only one instance when a crew lost their lives. It happened at night during the winter when one of our Ansons ditched in the sea within sight of Ramsay on the Isle of Man. A policeman on the dock was alerted by the sound of whistles, which all airmen carried and, realising what had happened, summoned help. Sadly, by the time their dinghy was reached, they were found to have died from exposure. Ironically, the Staff/WOp was on his first trip since returning from his honeymoon. He might have escaped this untimely end had he not requested that he be moved from the top to the bottom of the ops ladder because of his marriage. Who knows but that he might have survived a tour of operations had he not tampered with fate? A possible reason for the ditching was the failure to switch over to the spare fuel tanks. There were instances of this happening to others. But fortunately it was in daylight and the crews survived their ditchings.

A newly-fledged WOp/AG

Brothers three

My only hairy experience was while flying with a pilot on his first night solo. It was May '44 when we took off after midnight and were soon enveloped in cloud. As we climbed there were thumps on the aircraft – caused by lumps of ice being thrown from the propellers, and the windows became white with frost. Not only that, but the pilot called me over the intercom to say that he was having difficulty with the controls, the plane was slowing down and in danger of stalling, and what should we do? And I was the wireless op! My advice was that we should try to climb out of it and that meantime everyone should don their parachutes. I then sent a message to base, telling them of our predicament, and another to the coastguard so that they could fix our position. But this last was useless because the trailing aerial had iced up so that there was no transmission on the appropriate frequency band. However, to our great relief we broke cloud and saw in the distance a light flashing the code of the airfield at Millom where, ironically, the pilot had trained for his present job. He decided to land there to get our breath back and for a weather report. Strangely, of the dozen or so Ansons which had taken off at the same time, ours was the only one to encounter icing conditions. On looking back, it would have been suicide to parachute, as it would have been into the Irish Sea. I think I was more scared by that incident than by the trip to Berlin on September 3 the year before.

This happened as the result of a call for anyone wishing to experience a few days' detachment to an operational squadron. As I said previously, I was bored and looking for some action – and I got it!

I arrived to join 61 Squadron based at Syerston, near Nottingham, and shared a room with a WOp/AG who had been sick and had been replaced by another when his crew went on a trip to Berlin. They did not return! A day or so later I was asked if I would like to join a crew on one of the Lancasters scheduled for an unknown destination that night and I accepted. So I joined a crew with an NZ pilot, F/O Woods, and was informed the target for the night was Berlin!

Once on the aircraft, the W/Op was very helpful, seating me on the step beside him and showing me the connections for the intercom and oxygen supply. We were going to be climbing to 19,000 feet. Soon I heard the navigator announce that we were approaching the Dutch coast. And so we droned on until there was a panic shout over the intercom from the tailgunner that he wasn't getting oxygen, a most serious matter at this height and nearing the target. The W/Op turned hurriedly to me and indicated that I should clamber back and plug the tailgunner's oxygen tube in to an emergency tube about three-quarters of the way down the fuselage towards the turret. He slung an oxygen bottle around my shoulders which I plugged on to my mask, and clambered over the main spar and through the heavy metal door which the W/Op closed behind me. In blackness and with torch in hand I searched for the oxygen socket and the long tube plugged into it. Finding and connecting it I passed it quickly to the tailgunner and started back to my station. Reaching the dangling feet of the mid-upper gunner, and feeling a bit weak, I still had to scramble over a shiny metal surface covered with hydraulic fluid from the gun turret's recuperator so that I could reach the door and push it open. But I just didn't have the strength. However, the W/Op must have been timing me, for he opened the door, pulled me in and connected me to an oxygen outlet. No-one had told me that there was just ten minutes' supply of oxygen in the bottle!

A device for locating an approaching aircraft was an electronic beam around the craft which when entered produced a sequence of bleeps into one's headset. These increased in frequency as the aircraft drew nearer. Since it didn't differentiate between a friendly bomber and an enemy fighter, its use was limited. But the gunners could tell which was which by the number of engines with glowing exhausts. Two engines usually meant it was a deadly JU88 Luftwaffe Nightfighter.

So, having recovered from my oxygen ordeal, I was disturbed by a bleeping which got faster and faster. Next the tailgunner shouted: 'Corkscrew! Corkscrew!' and as the plane suddenly dived to port I involuntarily left my seat and found my head in the astrodome then was back in my seat again as it levelled out; this was followed by another excursion upwards, and as I descended this time it was into a cloud of Window, the silver strips that were to be chucked out to confuse enemy radar. Boxes of Window had lain by the navigator, who was similarly covered. However, as we neared the target he gathered what he could and pushed them down the flare chute. A few minutes later we arrived – and as the plane lifted suddenly, I knew the bomb load was on its way. Looking down and around I was dazzled by lights of all colours – this was Hell on Earth. Quickly the aircraft banked and headed north towards Sweden where, as we approached, the Swedes fired a few shots from anti-aircraft guns to cheer us on our way home. This was not to be as soon as expected, though, for a signal came through diverting us to Linton-on-Ouse to avoid German intruders who were circling Syerston, awaiting our return. It was about ten a.m. before we got back to base, where I was met by my room-mate who said he'd thought "the poor b--------" had bought it on his first trip.

Three nights later I joined another crew on a trip to Munich. This was entirely uneventful. And so back to Wigtown. Sometime later I was to hear snatches of a broadcast recorded by the BBC's Wilfred Vaughan Thomas while he flew on the same Berlin operation.

Back at Wigtown, I described, with due modesty, my hairy experiences to those who showed an interest. Among them was Johnny, who was later grounded with ear trouble and posted to either Kinross or Dalcross. I wasn't to meet him again till after the War when we bumped into each other at Easter Road after watching a Hibs match. He was back to his painting and decorating business.

I was to remain at Wigtown until the following July, 1944 – and during these months had some good and not so good experiences. Soon after my return from Syerston I was flattered by the station CO, Group Captain MacDonald, selecting me as his W/Op during a short visit to N. Ireland. Later, his second-in-command, Wing-Commander Coote, and I flew above the airfield on an exercise concerned with staging descent in bad weather. However, I was next to appear before the CO in a different role, i.e. on a charge of smoking in an aircraft – never mind that American aircraft had ashtrays fitted as standard – smoking was not permitted on any RAF planes, especially fabric-covered types, as was the Anson. It appeared that a Flight-Lieutenant, a former school-teacher, had instructed the WAAF cleaners that they should thoroughly sweep out all the aircraft flying on a particular day before they took off – and on their return they were to be checked for cigarette ash. Subsequently it was alleged that a tube of ash had been found in the wireless compartment of the Anson I'd flown in. As it happened, I had no intention of having a cigarette that day, and it was only when Tony, my regular pilot, passed his packet back, that I and the others aboard succumbed. Fortunately for me, the evidence was regarded as being too flimsy, as witnessed by the WAAFs involved with the alleged finding. They were on my side and, I gathered, supported my denial, which was of course a lie. In any event, having been marched in at double time to the CO's office, where the Group Captain questioned both myself and the Flight-Lieutenant, the coroner came to the conclusion that (in his own words) "Flight-Lieutenant ... had been out to catch someone smoking and had made a balls of it – case dismissed!". That was the one and only time I was on a charge during my five years' service, I'm pleased to say.

Still, there were some occasions when the WAAFs who cleaned the aircraft were not so supportive. The one I remember most had its origin in the "piss tube". Flying at around 4000 feet for four hours or so in an unheated plane, especially in winter, there would be an urgent need to empty bladders. So a metal funnel was available, to which was attached a tube running to an extension underneath, with the open end facing the tail. In time the underside fabric would become encrusted, and the WAAFs objected to having to clean it. As discouragement they would turn the pipe around 180 degrees so that the exit faced the slipstream, with the result that users got their own back! At such times I would hang on to a strut with one hand, open the door to the outside with the other and spray whatever lay below. It became easy with practice, but only became necessary when failing to check the position of the pipe before boarding.

There were many high-spirited jinks in the NCOs' quarters, one favourite having to do with beds. On one occasion a W/Op returning to his room after night flying found his bed missing. It was some time before he located it on the roof of his hut. Another stunt was to gently lift up a bed with soundly sleeping occupant and put it down by the side of the roadway into the camp for all arrivals from the early morning train to gawk at. Embarrassing and a trifle cruel, perhaps, but usually to celebrate the victim's birthday or some such event.

Being stationed at Wigtown, which was closer to home, made short leaves quite feasible. One such time stands out in my memory, and it was when I was returning from a long weekend. To get to Newton Stewart from Edinburgh by train one had to go to Carlisle and change to the train from the south going to Stranraer. It was called the boat train, with most of the passengers going to N. Ireland. It was winter and pitch black outside as we passed what I thought was Castle Douglas, though uncertain, because all stations were blacked out except for dim signal lights. About that time the guard came shouting through the passage "Next stop Stranraer!" and disappeared up the train before I could question him. Immediately panic set in. How could I get back from Stranraer, 25 miles further on, in time to catch the early morning train to Kirkinner? I was in a quandary until I remembered how, on its approach to the Newton Stewart station, the train reduced its speed to walking pace. Could I jump off as it reached the platform? Sure enough, the train slowed, slower and slower, and eventually, my head out of the door at the end of the corridor, I could see red and green signal lights, then the platform. So with my goon bag over my shoulder, I opened the door and prepared to jump out. Fortunately this desperate action wasn't necessary, for the train suddenly shuddered to a halt. Was this for my benefit? I don't think so, for as I walked towards the engine I saw its crew detach a hose from the adjacent water-tower and fix it to an inlet pipe. Perhaps this was a last-minute decision. But why wasn't the guard informed?

Finally, I enjoyed my 14 months in Wigtown, during which time I'd flown some 380 hours in daytime and 210 hours at night. I left in July '44, for OTU at Bicester, to train on Mitchells, the American B45 twin-engined medium bomber.

On the way to target

This Mitchell has a turret underneath as opposed to versions with guns in a position in the tailplane.

Soon after arriving at Bicester all personnel, pilots, navigators, WOp/AGs and gunners assembled for crew selection. It was up to each pilot to select the members he favoured. So Bob Dickson, a coloured Jamaican, picked a Glaswegian, Mac MacMillan, for navigator, Jack Warren, a Londoner, as his mid-upper gunner, and since no wireless operating was needed on these aircraft,

100

communication being by voice VHF, I became the fourth member as gunner, somewhere around the back of the plane, behind the bomb bay. A strange situation after all my wireless experience and extremely limited gunnery training – but who was I to argue? I was soon going to be flying on ops over occupied territory, in broad daylight, a fearful thought, with visions of the Gestapo below in my mind.

After a period of roughly four weeks and 30 hours' flying, during which time we flew various exercises, mainly for the pilot to become familiar with the Mitchell, we were posted to join a squadron. This was 320 Royal Dutch Naval Air Squadron, based at Dunsfold near Guildford. Representative crews from the Canadian, Australian and Belgian Air Forces, as well as the RAF, were also attached. This was because the Dutch had had many losses and didn't have enough Dutch replacements. Within a week of our arrival we took part in our first sortie and our target was troop concentrations at Abbeville. Later that day the target was marshalling yards at Givet, Belgium.

To relate individual targets covering the period September to the end of the War the following May would be boring for myself and the reader, considering how we carried out 53 sorties in that time. Suffice to say we aimed for troop concentrations, marshalling yards, bridges and strong points defended by the Germans. There were, however, some sorties of special interest in my memory. One was when heading for a target in Holland on Sunday morning, September 7, we overtook masses of aircraft towing gliders, on their way to the ill-fated operation that was Arnhem. We couldn't see our target for cloud so, being above occupied territory, with the possibility of our bombing allied civilians, we were recalled, bombs and all.

It's not a pleasant sensation landing with a full bomb load, but everyone landed without mishap. We did have to circle the airfield one evening when one of our planes with a bomb hang-up exploded as it touched down on the runway. It so happened that we'd planned to spend that evening in the bright lights of London and we were impatient with the time it took to clear the flaming debris so that we could land. How callous of us when I think about it now. It was not a plane from our squadron, so we didn't know the unfortunate crew who perished – but still....

Our squadron did suffer a few casualties, mainly from flak, for thankfully the Luftwaffe was rarely seen during the last months of the conflict. Strange as it may seem, the self-deprecation of myself as a gunner and thus the fear of coming to grips with enemy fighters far outweighed my fear of flak. To see the sudden glow of red flame and the puff of grey smoke from bursting shells seemed too distant and in some respects a game played between us and the youthful German gunners shooting from below. However, when one saw, as I did, Mitchells on fire and heading for the ground and escaping crews falling fast over the target with parachute canopies also aflame, I realised just how deadly flak could be.

It was on one such occasion as we were on our bomb run that the pilot instructed me to count the bombs as they left. This was uniquely possible because this particular version of the Mitchell had two 0.5 guns mounted in a ventral turret fitted behind the bomb doors. I could sight the guns through a periscope and rotate the contraption through 360 degrees. A spot of oil on the lens could cause unnecessary alarm, though. Was I seeing an enemy fighter? Anyway, I lined my guns so that they pointed to the bomb doors and proceeded to count the bombs as they dropped. Suddenly there was a bump. Oh, no, I thought, surely my guns haven't been struck by the tail-fin of one of the bombs. I pictured two guns, bent and pointing to the ground. What would the ground staff who maintained them have to say when we landed. They were Javanese and rather dour individuals.

However, as we neared our base I saw that a large section of the tailplane was missing and realised with some relief that this was the source of the bump. When I reported it to the pilot he was amazed as it hadn't affected the plane's handling.

So what was it that caused the damage? An unexploded shell, for they had proximity fuses which caused them to burst at a predetermined height? Or was it caused by a bomb dropped by an aircraft overhead? It will never be known. However, I was saved the embarrassment of right-angled gun barrels, which to me was more important.

Another version of Mitchell brought images to mind of valiant American Air Force gunners hosepiping the enemy and empty cartridge cases piling up at their feet. This version had guns sticking out through both sides of the plane, supported by pulley arrangements. It seemed a bit gungho and planned for two gunners, not for one poor soul to man both. Anyway, it's doubtful whether an enemy fighter would oblige by passing the position I was standing at. The best and most up-to-date model had two guns poking out through a cowling in the tail. The gunner sat on a low saddle with his knees on the floor and had a perfect vision – covering 180 degrees and able to look back towards the target while others approached it and dropped their bombs. We flew in a box of six aircraft flying in V-formation and packed together as tightly as possible to achieve maximum impact on the bombing point. The leader in the front V voiced his instruction to the others by counting down to the point of bombs release. Usually each squadron put up twelve aircraft for a sortie or eighteen for a maximum effort. 320 Squadron had to borrow planes on such occasions and on one of these this led to some acrimony between me and mid-upper Jack.

We flew in a borrowed plane of a neighbouring squadron and having bombed the target amid heavy flak which we were lucky to avoid, started for home. As we got nearer I got out of the rear turret and happened to notice that the housings for Jack's and my parachutes were empty. Suddenly it dawned on me that where in our squadron the 'chutes weren't removed, this was not the practice of the crews of the RAF squadron, who always carried their 'chutes to and from the aircraft. Poor Jack, he was livid and gave the impression that it was my fault, meaning in effect that we shouldn't have gone on to the target without them. I didn't argue but made sure to check next time we flew in a borrowed aircraft.

Jamaican Bob Dickson - Pilot,
Londoner Jack Warren - Gunner,
Self - Gunner, Belgian 'Snowy' - Navigator,
Javanese groundstaff, Melsbroek 1944

The squadrons were transferred to Melsbroek, now Belgium's international airport, near Brussels. With the Allied Armies so far ahead it made sense to station us nearer to them and the targets they called for. The move took place in the middle of October, 1944, and within a few days we were back to business.

One of our most persistent targets was the rail-bridge over the River Maas at Venlo, near the Dutch-German border. It was a suspension bridge and, as usual, difficult to down. The bombs went straight through it. Under cover of darkness the Germans would make it navigable by putting boards across the damage. Fifty years later, while on an exchange holiday, my wife Ann and I visited Venlo as part of a train excursion. A massive new steel bridge crossed the Maas to the town from Blerick, a village on the opposite bank, a village which also brought back memories. Sitting in sunshine outside a café eating ice-cream while the residents and visitors of Venlo hastened or strolled around under our gaze, with no sign whatsoever of bomb damage, I could only imagine the different scene half a century before when we flew over.

In January, '45, while on an exchange attachment to the Yorkshire and Lancashire Light Infantry, which was then an airborne regiment and had taken part in the Ardennes battle over Christmas and New Year, and now held the line at Blerick opposite the Germans at Venlo, I had a third view. I went with a party led by a lieutenant to the river bank, where sappers laid trip-wires to alert them to any German patrols which might cross over. It was night-time and pitch black although the ground was snow-covered. While sitting with one of the squaddies, Bren gun at the ready, I saw a German sentry light up a cigarette. We were that close, as he patrolled outside a large building on the Venlo side. Apparently a battalion of Royal Scots had been in this sector before the YOLIs had relieved them, and had lost some men from outpost positions to German patrols which had crossed over. I must say I found this experience of being opposite the enemy while ground-borne as opposed to airborne a bit eerie. I felt like a fish out of water. It seems to me that the Liverpudlian lieutenant, a peace-time lawyer, was pulling my leg when he outlined the original planned objective of the patrol before we set off. This was for us to cross the river in a dinghy, and on reaching the bank for some to form a spearhead, followed by others in a similar but reverse formation behind, while I would be in the middle. At the first sign of opposition those forward would open fire then change places with the others and keep leap-frogging back to the dinghy. It seemed a bit daunting – but if they were prepared to fly on sorties with our squadron, and some did, why should I shirk this experience? However, I was not too disappointed at what seemed to me then a change of plan. Not a shot fired, and the bonus of some chickens caught running loose in the farmyard close to our position.

I spent that night billeted in a bungalow in the village, sleeping on a camp bed beside the kitchen door. Dick, who had accompanied me from the squadron, had a double bed to himself. He, a Dutch Navy lieutenant and navigator, was married to an Englishwoman and had a young child. For this reason he had refused the invitation to join what appeared to be a hazardous patrol. Anyway, I was disturbed from my sleep and on opening my eyes saw a light coming from the partly open door at the other side of the room. As the door opened wider there was a square Germanic face looking towards me which suddenly uttered: Zo! Surely it was only Germans who make such an announcement? Quietly I reached for my revolver and slipped it under the covers with my finger on the trigger. Just then the figure, wearing a dog-collar, approached, stepped over my bed, entered the kitchen and put the kettle on. He was a priest on his way to Mass.

The battalion's HQ was centred in a convent, still occupied by the Father (not the same one) and a few nuns. While we were there a nun came down to the make-shift cook-house from upstairs and said that the Father had a cold and could he have some whisky? He got it, of course, as he had before, along with cigarettes. What appalled me here was that while the locals were foraging in the waste bins outside for scraps to eat, there were dozens of milk churns packed full with pickled eggs covering the whole floor of the convent's basement. However, the army boys treated us well – but after a few days in their company, sharing their discomfort in the cold, snowy conditions that prevailed at the time and the risks of patrolling on the front line, I returned to the squadron glad that I'd joined the RAF.

Apart from this excursion, most of January, February and March were spent on sorties against targets in front of our troops as they advanced towards the Rhine. In April the squadron transferred to a former Luftwaffe airfield at Achmer near Osnabrück. We flew three sorties from here to Bremen and Hamburg. Then our job was done, for on May 5th peace was declared, as announced by Winston Churchill over the radio. This had seemed inevitable, for only a few days before, while I was outside the tent I shared, having a shave, a large black four-engined plane appeared. I was baffled, for it looked like a Dakota but for the number of engines. It was, in fact, a Focke-Wolf Condor, a long-range type used over the Atlantic. This one had flown from its base in Norway to surrender.

On landing, the crew were met by a delegation of armed officers and men who led them away, despite their pleas to be allowed to return to their homes. No doubt they would have been interrogated and held prisoner for a while.

Posing in front of abandoned German aircraft, at Melsbroe

JIM FERGUSON   MICKEY WALKER   MAC MACMILLAN   BOB DANSKIN
NAVIGATOR,   WOP/AG   NAVIGATOR   WOP/A.G
GREENOCK?   YORKSHIRE   GLASGOW   EDINBURGH

A week later we were to have our last flight on Mitchells when we set off on a special mission along with a Mitchell crewed by Australians. It seemed that U-boats carrying Nazi dignitaries to safety in S. America were making their way through the Baltic and that Mosquitoes were to be sent to intercept them. First, though, they would have to land and refuel at the airfield near Lubeck. So our task, along with ground staff aboard, was to land earlier and put goose flares on the runway edges to guide them in, since it would be dark. However, we were warned that it might not be so straightforward because of possible danger from

Werewolves, the name given to young, fanatical Nazis who could not accept defeat and were armed. The plan was that after landing we should quickly leave our aircraft and, using the trenching tools we carried, dig in and have our revolvers, rifles or whatever at the ready. All being clear, work on the lights could begin.

An hour after leaving Achmer we were over Lubeck – and to our relief, consternation and delight we saw many RAF Typhoons on the ground, which we learned later had arrived nearly a week before. So much for Intelligence! Anyway, we enjoyed ourselves careering around in a commandeered German version of a Jeep and the forerunner of the Volkswagen Beetle. We saw what seemed an endless line of German army, navy and airforce prisoners walking from the docks, having disembarked from the ships that had brought them from Norway. One squaddy at the front with slung rifle and one or two others similarly armed ambled alongside, safe in the knowledge that none was in the mood to make a break for it. Our flight back to base included a Cook's tour of the Ruhr and the devastation wrought by years of bombing of this industrial sector of Germany.

Apart from the flying side of it, a number of other events stand out in my memory. One occurred on New Year's Day, '45, when Hitler sent hundreds of planes over Belgium and Holland in a last-gasp attempt to neutralise Allied airforces on airfields there, his ambitious break through the Ardennes towards Antwerp and the coast having been foiled, with his troops at a standstill or in retreat well short of their planned targets.

By coincidence, the Mitchell squadrons were assembled for another maximum effort that morning and once again we were allocated a borrowed plane. As luck would have it, Bob said that it was unserviceable. And while the rest of the squadron headed off to their target we retired to the crew room, where we

stretched out on benches and tables to catch up on lost sleep. After all it had been Hogmanay and we'd seen in the New Year.
Suddenly there was the rattling of machine-gun fire and the roar of aircraft engines. Jumping up, I ran to the door to see what was going on, when a Messerschmidt 109 crossed my vision, flying no higher than twenty feet. There were others zooming around and firing. Then, as quickly as it had started, the noise stopped. The motley collection of bombers and fighters had left for another target airfield. How fortunate that the thirty-six bomb-laden Mitchells had gone a matter of minutes before! The chap who controlled the take-off and landing of aircraft from a caravan at the start of the runway had a scare, though. He thought the fast-approaching Messerschmidt was a Spitfire and flashed red because it was heading for the runway that was not in use. A quick burst from the "Spitfire's" guns soon had him scurrying under the caravan. The damage to various types of unserviceable aircraft on the ground was minimal.

Then there was the question of Hitler's secret weapons - V1 pilotless planes loaded with explosives, and the V2 rocket, which reached a height of fifty thousand feet before descending on London. I became involved with both of these lethal weapons in various situations.

My first encounter was on the way from home to the training course near Hereford. I was travelling with another WOp/AG who had been with me at Wigtown and whose parents lived at South Croydon. Since we had a day or so to spare before joining the course he invited me to stay overnight at his home. One could say that this was more of a challenge than a hospitable gesture, for the house was situated in Bomb Alley, so called for the number of V1s landing in the strip leading to Croydon aerodrome and beyond. The house and its neighbours didn't have a whole window-pane left, while outside doors had to be propped up after being blasted off their hinges. Although a number of V1s, or flying bombs, as they were called, passed overhead during my stay there, they kept on going. One took cover when the noise of the engine stopped abruptly. Then there was silence, followed by a loud explosion when the missile dived to the ground.

Brussels too was a target. I can remember when Prince Bernhardt was presenting medals to fellow Dutch members of the squadron as they lined up on the airfield. Soon a V1 approached with its familiar crackling sound. Fortunately it passed overhead and a few seconds elapsed before the engine cut out and it exploded. Meanwhile the ceremony continued regardless.

I had made friends with Janine, a local girl who took me home to meet her family, all of whom could speak English of sorts. The grandmother was a cause for concern because she had been caught by the Gestapo and taken to Germany for harbouring RAF escapees in her house some months before. Anyway, because of the hour and the curfew, I was invited to stay the night and slept on a couch in a ground-floor room. Later this invitation was repeated but I had to decline because I was on the Battle Order for next morning. Which was just as well, for a flying bomb had landed in the street that night, demolishing the room, including the couch. Sadly, I lost touch with Janine and her family because of a communications misunderstanding. So I never did learn of the grandmother's fate. C'est la guerre!

One afternoon, soon after take-off, and as we were forming into our usual boxes of six aircraft on our way to a target, all the aircraft suddenly dropped from the sky. Seconds passed before we recovered. The only explanation that we could come up with for this unusual event was that we had been caught in the slipstream of an ascending V2 rocket. It certainly gave everyone quite a scare.

With the end of the European War and my contribution, I was soon on my way home by Dakota from Evert, Belgium's International Airport before the War, to Northolt, followed by a pleasant train journey in the company of a group of ex-POWs, most of whom were Australian soldiers captured at Tobruk and held in Italy – now heading for Edinburgh for a spell of leave before the long voyage home.

With Jack and Pat, former POWs captured at Tobruk, and brother David

I befriended two of them, Pat, a former railway train fireman of Irish ancestry, and Jack, of German stock, who had been a cowboy, though it was sheep he'd rounded up. They were most generous and gifted me a couple of cartons of cigarettes and shared their booze from the gunny-sacks they carried, which seemed to be full of the stuff. It had been given them by Australia House or some such grateful institution. On arriving in Edinburgh I invited them home for breakfast. They stayed for two weeks.

Soon I was on my way to the Aircrew Allocation Centre at Catterick in Yorkshire. Here RAF aircrew from the various commands engaged in the now ended European War were assessed for other duties. Pop had advised me to opt for further education with a view to qualifying for entry to university, so I made an appropriate appointment. However, all seemed very vague in that direction so I applied to continue flying and following a successful medical I was accepted for training as W/Op with Transport Command and posted to the Conversion Unit at Bramcote near Nuneaton.

The course was intensive, with a great deal of flying on Dakotas on cross-country days and nights, for a total of 73 hours. To complete the course successfully, W/Ops had to be able to send and receive (in Morse Code) at a minimum of 25 words a minute. I managed 30 wpm. Part-way through the course, word came of the dropping of the atom bombs and the Japanese surrender. At this we were sent on home leave while the RAF decided what to do with us.

I had palled-up with another W/Op called Les Smith from Aberdeen and we decided that since we'd just returned from leave shortly before we'd visit a few places we'd never been to, such as Grimsby (grim), Coventry (badly bomb-damaged, including the cathedral) and Sheffield, where we spent a couple of days, mainly in the Round bar. This was a novelty, with an ex-Battle of Britain pilot (alleged) who greeted all who entered with a kiss for the ladies, usually WAAFs, and an invitation to all comers to participate in Cardinal Puff. Here one had to down a pint of beer in one go to an accompanying dirge and chanting of chug-a-lug, repeated until the glass had been emptied. Success gave the privilege of sitting comfortably in a fenced-off section with tables, one of which was called the Cow Pasture for obvious reasons, while failure meant the purchase by the victim of drinks all round. So there was every incentive to succeed. As you'd expect, my Aberdonian friend succeeded, as did I. At a later date we were to celebrate the end of the War with Japan, VJ Day, in Leicester, amid the throng gathered at the County buildings. I slept that night on a table in the YMCA. Our course was over by the end of October, 1944 and both Les and I were promoted to Warrant Officer. And so to Morecambe, where we waited for our next posting.

After four weeks or so of idle days and hectic nights at the Floral Hall ballroom, we learned our fate. Les and I were going to India; he to Poona and I to Dum Dum, near Calcutta. I flew out as a passenger on a converted Stirling bomber, with overnight stops at Castel Benito in Libya, Lydda near Tel Aviv, Shaibah in Iraq, then on to Karachi where we changed to a Dakota. Stopping at Palam and Chakulia on the way, we finally arrived at Dum Dum and 52 Squadron. We had a narrow squeak, though, just escaping a week's jungle survival course, suggested by an over-zealous officer at Chakulia, no doubt looking for something to justify his employment now that the War was ended. He did manage to palm off various items of surplus stores in his keeping, such as calf-length boots with suede uppers and leather soles; protection against snakes? They lay at home, unworn, for years afterwards. Someone must have decided that our services were required more urgently with the squadron than cavorting in the bush.

Until recently, this squadron of Dakotas, in conjunction with USAF squadrons, had carried arms and other supplies across the Hump, as the Himalayas were described, to Chungking in China. Initially this operation was to assist the regime of the Chinese leader, Chiang Kai Shek, in his fight against the Japanese and it had continued for a while after the surrender to counter the Communists under Mao Tse Tung. Flying Dakotas over the Hump was extremely hazardous from all accounts, with a high number of losses. So I was not too disappointed to have missed the opportunity to visit China under these circumstances. I believe some of the supplies so transported were for the Americans, who were supporting the Vietnamese in their fight, not only against the Japanese, but the French forces who as a part of the Vichy regime had allied themselves with the enemy. Very ironic, as it turned out, considering the Americans' role a few years later in the Vietnamese War.

The squadron personnel occupied a former girls' school by the road leading from the city of Calcutta to the airfield at Dum Dum, where the infamous bullet of that name had been manufactured. I shared a tent with three English second pilots with little flying experience to talk of – though they did! Still, we got on well enough and, in fact, on returning to the UK for demob later, I carried an engagement ring given to me by one of them and posted it from home to his fiancée. They did annoy me one night though, when disturbed by the noise from across the road where an Indian wedding was being celebrated. They shouted for the guests to keep quiet and emphasised this by throwing stones in their direction. I was to find the same overbearing reaction to the "natives" much later while resident in Hong Kong and found it equally distasteful.

It was fully four weeks since leaving the UK before I joined a crew for our first trip but it was a few trips later before I settled with a permanent pilot and navigator, both of whom had been policemen and were called Eric and Percy, respectively. I can't recall the role played previously by Eric, but Flight-Lieutenant Percy had flown with Wing-Commander Tait while bombing the disabled German battleship *Tirpitz* as she lay in a Norwegian fjord. Their aircraft shot up, they limped to Sweden and were later flown home to the UK in a converted Mosquito.

Our function was that eventually performed by commercial

airlines – the transport of passengers, mail and cargo to airfields as far apart as Bombay and Hong Kong. We were the link to heavier aircraft such as the York, which flew the first leg from the UK to Dum Dum, via New Delhi. To look the part, we wore white overalls with the squadron badge on the pocket.

On one occasion I panicked just before take-off when I discovered, on retrieving my laundry from the dhobi-wallah, that the clean overalls I was depending on wearing were a delicate shade of pink! Not daring to wear these, I had to dash around looking for someone to lend me a set. I must have been successful for the flight wasn't delayed.

I enjoyed being the W/Op on a Dakota. The equipment was more sophisticated than I had been accustomed to on RAF aircraft, a feature being the trailing aerial which could be reeled in or out at the touch of a button instead of being laboriously wound manually. It was quite an adventure, and educational too, touching down at places with such exotic names as Chittagong, Mecktila, Hmawbi, Bangkok, Saigon, Rangoon, Nagpur, Singapore, Penang and, as previously mentioned, Bombay and Hong Kong. Percy and I even had a trip as reliefs for sick crew members on a Dakota containing two replacement engines to Batavia (Jakarta) in Java, now Indonesia. A bit disastrous this one, for I got into a fight with a sailor who objected to my criticism of his row of medal ribbons. (The navy had only to sail through hostile waters to qualify, while aircrew in the RAF, whether in Bomber Command or my previous outfit, the 2nd Tactical Airforce, received no recognition other than the campaign medals given to everyone who crossed the Channel into Europe.) The fracas took place at the Black Cat, a pub to which I'd been taken by a Glaswegian navigator whose crew I was temporarily billeted with. It was his birthday.

Having a leisurely day in Singapore before returning by slip plane to Dum Dum

Outside the tent I lived in and shared with the three second pilots standing alongside. This is near Dum Dum.

As an officer, Percy had been billeted elsewhere and he too had had his problems when, in the dark, he wandered into a monsoon ditch. Muddied and without his cap, and I not looking too good either, we got a lift to Singapore, spent a night at a transit camp in Rangoon and gratefully arrived next day back at Dum Dum. Two days later we were delivering supplies to the usual stopping places in Burma and Bangladesh.

We had a bearer, a young Indian who went on errands and tidied the tent. One day I sent him to the durzi-wallah (tailor) to have my medal ribbons sewn onto a new khaki drill jacket. I gave him a couple of rupees to cover the cost. You can imagine my anger when he handed back the "finished" job with the ribbons upside-down and held with large stitches of black thread. Needless to say he hadn't been to the tailor, but I made sure that he did go after that and with due haste. After that and other incidents we decided to replace the bearer with, hopefully, a more efficient and honest one. So we sent out word about our quest. One likely lad appeared and eagerly thrust a note into my hand – a letter of recommendation from another airman, he said. On opening it, I read, "This bearer would make a f....... good banjo player!" He wasn't hired.

Meals when we weren't away were served in the school building. But between these we'd be alerted by the cry of the char-wallah. Humping a copper urn full of hot tea and a wicker basket containing cakes, he went from tent to tent and was usually welcomed by us growing lads. How he managed to keep the tea hot I can't remember, but I enjoyed it – and the cakes, which had the texture and appearance of rice biscuits and were semi-sweet. The city of Calcutta was worth a visit or two and we travelled to and fro on the back of an RAF ghari (truck) which ran a regular shuttle service. This was preferable to, and safer than, taxis driven with gay abandon by large bearded Sikhs who frequently coasted slowly past our residences with gesturing prostitutes aboard. I never saw any takers.

Chowringee is the main thoroughfare which despite the War looked very presentable with solid buildings on one side and gardens on the other. I seem to remember seeing an open-air swimming pool in that area. Behind the buildings the main stalls of an open-air bazaar could be seen but I didn't venture far into it. There were beggars about and some pitiful sights too, but fortunately it wasn't the day when masses of them were allowed into the city.

I never felt that I was an aggressive type, yet once again I found myself engaged in fisticuffs. Len, one of the chaps in the tent, invited me to accompany him to a dance organised by some women's group – WRI or something – in a hall in Chowringee. Inside, we sat at a table with our drinks while viewing the dancers. After a while I noticed a pretty Eurasian girl returning to join some older women sitting at the side. When the music started up again I asked the girl up to dance, after which I returned her to her group, went back to our table, then to the toilet. "That corporal over there has taken your drink", Len said, and I with disbelief at such an action looked across to said RAF corporal who was with my dancing partner and her party. He then approached and started berating me for dancing with his girlfriend. More disbelief on my part, especially when he invited me to step outside. I agreed and followed him and two or three of his cronies towards the door leading to the street. On arriving he turned to face me with his back to the door – or the half of it that was still closed. So wasting no time I gave him what he asked for and went back to the table. However friend Len, all six feet two of him, had beaten a hasty retreat. I was then joined by one of the Eurasian women, presumably one of the girl's group, who blamed me for all that had happened. It seemed to me to be so unjustified that I left with a few choice words, just in time to catch the last ghari. My hero Len was asleep on my return and had little to say the next morning. He did inform me a few days later that the women's committee had banned me from their premises – as if I cared – though I did return once more and wasn't identified. Was this challenge by the corporal a case of jealousy on his part? Had Len said something to him that he'd resented and picked on me as the smaller one, or was he showing off? I'll never know. But I'm sure that he must have regretted his challenge.

The trips I enjoyed most were to Kai Tak airfield, Hong Kong. We flew via Hmawbi in Burma, to Bangkok, to Saigon, where we stayed overnight in a hotel and our bags were taken to our room by a uniformed Japanese POW, then on to Hong Kong. The total flying time for the journey was seventeen hours. How different HK was in those days shortly after the War!

The population could be numbered in thousands, compared to the six or seven million of today. There were very few tall buildings, while all the houses alongside the Peak tram route had been demolished. It was a tricky job to approach the airfield in low cloud, though, what with the tall buildings remaining and the closeness of the field to a mountain. On our first trip we arrived in such dodgy conditions that air traffic control said we should be prepared to divert to the White Cloud Airfield at Canton on the Chinese mainland. But we were a bit anxious about this since it was held by the Communists. Fortunately it cleared sufficiently before this became necessary and we landed at Kai Tak as planned – but with some trepidation, with buildings too close for comfort as our wing-tips passed them.

We stayed in a small hotel in Kowloon, venturing across to the island in the evening and into a dance-hall where one bought tickets which were exchanged for Chinese dancing partners – a so-called taxi dance. Many US Navy sailors were on the dance floor. On the stroke of midnight they had to leave and return to their ship. Dawdlers were hauled out by the Navy Police, belted with clubs and man-handled into paddy wagons.

A fond memory of my second visit to HK was of sitting in a posh restaurant with the others having brunch while a pianist played quietly nearby. He played "Claire de Lune" which I, hearing it for the first time, thought was marvellous. Next day, we took off on our return journey, refreshed and ready for the long trip back to Dum Dum, ignorant of the traumatic experience we'd encounter on the way.

Airborne at 7 am with a mixed bag of passengers, including military personnel and Chinese civilians plus mail, we made our way across the South China Sea, heading for Saigon. Suddenly, about one and a half hours from our ETA, the starboard engine cut out and the plane immediately started losing height. The weather had deteriorated during the flight and we'd experienced considerable turbulence, to the discomfort of the passengers. The sight of a slowly windmilling propeller in addition hardly raised the spirits! Normally in such a situation the pilot could feather the propeller of a faulty engine, which meant that it became fixed, with the blades angled forward to give the least resistance. With an aircraft such as the Dakota, it could then be flown quite comfortably on just one engine. However the feathering mechanism didn't respond in this instance. Whereupon I was instructed to send a message to Saigon informing them of our plight. My message was acknowledged by the Saigon operator and by another aircraft flying in the vicinity. At one time, because we were losing height so rapidly, it seemed that we'd have to ditch into the sea. Alternatively, there could have been the possibility of reaching the coastline 200 miles or so north-east of Saigon. Either choice would have been fraught with danger, especially with my memory of the fate of a French pilot who had baled out of his Spitfire and could be seen dangling from his parachute as we watched from the airfield. Later we were to learn that his rescuers found his body chopped to pieces by the Vietnamese.

Fortunately we were to avoid either possibility. Eric called back to say that he'd managed to get the propeller feathered and that we were gaining height. I sent this glad news abroad. In due course crew and passengers stumbled out of the aircraft on landing at Saigon, much relieved to be on firm ground. Imagine our astonishment, when, on reporting to the Control Tower, we discovered that the personnel there had been unaware of our problem because the W/Op, housed in a shack on the perimeter, hadn't advised them of my emergency message. Yet when we looked at his log, it was there. Eric was furious, but I never learned what, if any, action followed.

Anyway, we left the Dakota for repair and returned to Dum Dum as passengers on another. And so ended my flying in the Far East.

That invigorating episode over, it was now time to pack my gear in preparation for my return journey to the UK and Civvy Street. On the first stage I and many aircrew types joined a train at the Calcutta railway station and, laden with packets of K rations, were all set for the two-day crossing of the continent to Bombay and the transit camp at Worli. It was an open carriage and I shared a space with three others, sitting at or resting on pull-down beds. On looking down the carriage one faced other chaps housed in the same arrangement. At the various stops on the way we were able to get water for tea from the engine boiler. So even under the trying circumstances of such a long journey we were quite comfortable. The contents of the boxes of K rations – tins of cheese, spam, tea etc., became boring, so much so that we helped relieve the undernourished Indian peasants working in the fields we passed through by tossing out tins to them as we sped along.

On arriving at the transit camp we mingled with those who'd arrived previously and there were many reunions. Some hadn't seen each other from years before when they had been together at different stages of training or in different commands. There was a lot of enthusiastic back-thumping and hand-shaking. I had my turn when I found my arm being pumped up and down and being greeted by the question, "Where did I see you before?". How could I reply but to say truthfully that we had been facing one another down the carriage of the train we'd just left!

Anyway, we were soon on the *Georgic* troopship on our way to Liverpool via Aden and the Suez Canal. Within three weeks I was home in Edinburgh, having parted with items of uniform in exchange for a civvy suit, overcoat and split-pea hat. In addition, I had a brown suit of woollen texture which, although ready-made, fitted me like a glove. I'd bought it in Calcutta.

Like most ex-servicemen I didn't find settling back in civilian life easy. However I returned to the Post Office about two months after my discharge – this time as a sorter and later as a counter clerk at the GPO. When I learned that there was a call for recruits to join the RAF Volunteer Reserve at Scone, where W/Ops could fly on exercises on Ansons at weekends and during a two-week period each year, I applied and was accepted. This was about three years later, in March, 1949.

By now the Anson was a different aircraft in that it had a metal covering as opposed to fabric. The entry door was now on the port side while the interior was compartmentalised on the starboard side. Otherwise it was the same old dependable plane I'd flown over 600 hours in.

The training programmes for pilots and W/Ops was the responsibility of civilian staff employed by Airwork. The VR pilots flew Tiger Moths and Chipmunks.

Flying around Scotland for two and a half hours on average on a Sunday, with little to do other than make contact with ground stations, hardly had the adrenalin pumping. Only the mandatory two weeks' annual camp could be interesting. On two occasions a few of us flew to Jersey for a couple of nights, each time staying at what was known as the "honeymoon hotel". When it was suggested that I should join the Strathtay Aero Club with a view to qualifying for a Private Pilot's Licence and the possibility of re-mustering to pilot in the Reserve, I jumped at the chance. I had to pay for the lessons myself, of course.

In 1950 I spent two weeks at Transport Command HQ at Lyneham, Wilts. During this time I was fortunate to be included with a crew flying a Hastings to Fayid, by the Suez Canal, via Luqa in Malta, and El Adam. We spent the afternoon and evening in Valetta before setting off next day on the other legs. We returned by the same route, after spending a night at the isolated airfield, with WAAFs and airmen as passengers.

Though this was enjoyable, my impression of the peacetime RAF was such that I included a number of criticisms in my report to my CO back in Scone and said that any thoughts I'd had of rejoining had been shattered. I described the situation in the Sergeants' Mess, where anarchy reigned in the kitchens staffed by National Service airmen – who I'd seen ignoring the Station Warrant Officer, who had to wash his own cutlery while a couple argued and started fighting in his presence, without any reaction from him. Also, airmen wiped tables "clean" using old socks. I'm not sure I said how depressing it was to see NCO aircrew washing down aircraft prior to the Air Officer Commanding's inspection. Also how dead the Sergeants' Mess was, with crews away on trips or at home with their families outside on their return. It was not the RAF as I'd known it.

I started pilot training at the end of November 1950. But it wasn't till June '51 that I flew solo for the first time – and this after about fourteen hours with an instructor. Bad weather and a grass runway which led to unsuitable conditions were the main cause of this prolonged period before going solo. However after about forty hours I qualified for my licence.

The next step was to apply to remuster, and as an initial step the Chief Flying Instructor tested me in a Chipmunk and was satisfied with my ability. Sadly, I was later informed that at 29 years of age I exceeded the maximum age for pilot training with the RAF by four years. As luck would have it, I'd left the Post Office for Admiralty by this time and was working in London. And so ended my link with the RAF and flying until much later on civilian aircraft – as a passenger.

I enjoyed flying as a WOp/AG, despite my persistent yearning to be a pilot which, of course, I achieved in a small way by qualifying for a Private Pilot's Licence. As a gunner on Mitchells I felt out of place and with the Luftwaffe defeated to all intents and purposes by the end of '44, of only nominal use. After my Berlin experience in '43 I can only admire those aircrews of Bomber Command who night after night faced the same harrowing events, during which time German night fighters were extremely numerous and active. How would I have fared as a pilot? Who knows? Perhaps I was lucky to have been chosen as a WOp/Ag. I had flown over fifty sorties on Mitchells, the two operations on Lancasters, quite a number of trips on Dakotas, and of course many hours in Ansons, and survived unscathed.

RETURN TO CIVVY STREET

As I've already mentioned, in September '46, after three months' demob leave from the RAF, I returned to work in the GPO, this time as a Sorting Clerk and Telegraphist. Only the first half of that title was relevant. This was, of course, quite a change from my four years plus as an RAF "Glamour Boy" - but since one's peers were experiencing the same let-down, there seemed little else to do except buckle down to this new experience. The fact that the others had been boy messengers in an earlier age produced a certain cameraderie, which helped, but there were changes on the way. A major one was the introduction of a new type of postman, called Postman Higher Grade, recruited from the Outdoor branch of the PO Union. They kept their postmen's uniforms, while we wore a dustcoat. Unfortunately, where we mucked in to assist each other at times when an overload of mail caused one of us to have difficulty with meeting the deadline for having mail sorted and bagged for collection, in time for loading for particular train departures, the PHGs simply finished their stint and cleared off home. It was not unusual for us to help them out, for missing a deadline would result in severe repercussions for us all. Anyway, within about two years I and a number of other sorters were promoted to Postal and Telegraph Officer, another misnomer, when in fact the job entailed serving at the General Post Office counters.

In those days customers had an 8 am to 9 pm service, six days a week, and two hours on Sunday morning. And this for every day of the year, New Year's Day excepted. These were the days of football coupons, when masses would crowd into the hall to buy postal orders to send with their coupon. In between these fast transactions there were requests for money orders, telegraph money orders, licences for motor vehicles, guns and dogs, employment stamps and, of course, postage stamps. Parcels were handled at a separate counter. Which reminds me of a story.

The GPO counter was something like sixty feet long, with fifteen or so positions. It ran parallel to the street outside, the North Bridge. A wag called Andrew Logan was serving at the first position, reserved mainly for the sale of stamps and postal orders, when an old lady appeared, carrying a large parcel. When Andrew told her that the parcel counter was at the far end, she complained: "Have I got to walk away up there?". To which he replied: "You could always get a tram outside!". Obviously, I still find it funny!

There could be a lot of pressure at times, especially on Wednesdays and Thursdays, with people anxious to get their football pool coupons posted. Fast transactions such as postal orders were interspersed with slower ones for motor vehicle licences and telegraph money orders, so one's concentration was sorely taxed, especially with the babble of impatient types in one's ears. Still, as was said, one could only serve one customer at a time as he or she stood at your position. Since we had to balance our stock at the end of our shift, we didn't appreciate the flurry of customers who suddenly burst in ten minutes or less before closing time.

My time at the GPO counters was followed by a spell at Newington PO. The Postmistress, Miss Bland, was a benign soul, a middle-aged spinster not lacking in discipline, as she had to be, charged as she was with the control of four or five of us youngsters, all male. It was here that I learned how to prepare the daily Cash Account, which meant producing the previous day's office transactions on a balance sheet for the Finance Office in Lothian House. This was to stand me in good stead for I was later chosen to prepare the Cash Account for the GPO – a much bigger job of course. It involved all the transactions for the previous day's business at the GPO counters, i.e. the various pensions and allowances, stamps, money orders, postal orders etc. and the cash received. I prepared a double-entry cash account as previously, which I took to the Head Postmaster for his signature. As before, I then sent it to Lothian House. Strangely, although I had no difficulty carrying out this procedure, two of my predecessors at the job did and were known to work until midnight in order to achieve a balance. The hours were from 8 am to 4 pm but I was usually on my way home by 3.15 pm.

After a few months at this job I saw an advert in a Post Office publication inviting applications for a postal position at Livingston, Nyasaland. Having submitted my application through my boss, I waited patiently for a response. Some time later, as a result of the Civil Service exam I'd sat what seemed like years before, I was offered the post of Clerical Officer with Admiralty. For a number of reasons I decided to accept this offer. It seemed like promotion – and because it was Admiralty, I envisaged an opportunity for foreign travel. Also, there was talk of people in upstairs jobs like mine being returned to counter duties, thus making way for others. And I learned that my boss had not forwarded my application. When the Head Postmaster heard I was leaving he told me I'd be better advised to stay with the PO. Certainly, I favoured the idea of becoming Postmaster of a Border town – Hawick, Kelso or Peebles, for example – but that could have been years ahead, if ever. My boss worked in a strongroom behind my desk, which held many thousands of pounds' worth of postage stamps, postal orders etc. which he parcelled out to POs nationwide. Maybe he had it in mind for me to replace him on his retiral! Anyway, in March '52 I reported to the office of a director of Naval Accounts at Harrow-on-the-Hill, just along the way from Wembley Stadium.

Here I had a piddling sort of job checking invoices and receipts from Navy establishments around the world. I sat in a small cramped office with four or five others in a wooden hut – a sort of portacabin, a temporary war-time structure. A youngish girl sat opposite me, while to my left on a high stool sat a Dickensian character. He was short, fat and bald and seemed to spend most of his day alternately lighting his pipe, smoking cigarettes, inhaling snuff or doing something with balsam. This wasn't my scene and it was lightened only by Bill Cassels in the adjoining office – an ex-WOp/AG like myself, from Dumfries. We hit it off together, playing golf at Rayner's Lane and attending the local dance-hall, where beer was on tap. However, by August of that year we managed to get transferred to Rosyth Dockyard. Soon after, Bill left for a job with Post Office Telephone Sales. I attended his wedding at Blair Atholl, the home of his wife.

There was nothing appealing about this job either, preparing and issuing pay-packets to dockyard workers. I had let it be known that I was hoping for an overseas posting, so imagine my delight when the boss called down to me from his upstairs office asking if I'd like to go to Hong Kong.

HONG KONG REVISITED

So on the last day of January '53 I embarked on the *Chusan* for the month-long voyage.

For the first two weeks it was blissful. Plenty of food and drink (bread and sweets were still rationed at this time in the UK), lots of entertainment and a mingling of passengers of all nationalities, many of whom disembarked at our first port of call, Bombay. More were to leave at Colombo and then Singapore. By this time the ship was near empty, the entertainment had ceased and meals had lost their novelty. It was with relief that we reached our destination.

I had chummed up with a chap, MacKenzie by name, who worked with PO Telephones in Glasgow. His new job in HK was to seek out clandestine radio transmissions. This was to lead him into a number of hairy situations. Sometimes, accompanied by police, he would raid suspect premises to find that it was an opium den, with no evidence of wireless equipment.

Mac shared a government flat with Steve, a forty-year-old Assistant Government Librarian. Previously he'd been in Brunei. While Mac and I were active and making the most of what the colony had to offer on our meagre salaries, Steve would spend most of his leisure time reading, which follows, I suppose.

I had a room in the Admiralty Civilian Officers' Mess, in Kowloon. It was sparsely furnished but had a large bath and a balcony looking out to the street and overlooking Chinese-occupied houses. Tang, the head boy, served at the bar and had a staff who prepared the meals, did our laundry and carried out general housekeeping. It was quite a cosy and civilised set-up, although meals were sparse because of the paltry allowance for purchasing food from Navy Stores by Admiralty. We had to make up for extras on our Mess bill.

There were about twenty other residents representing the various disciplines to be found in a Navy Dockyard, such as the engineering and electrical departments where they ranked as supervisors or middle managers. Most were Englishmen from the South-East or the West Country and, as I learned once again, they showed the same disdain of the natives (Chinese) as had their countrymen in India. One of their number, Eric Brown, detested those Chinese who dismounted from their bike and wheeled it on and across the pavement, forcing pedestrians to come to a halt. This was a common show of bad manners which, when Eric encountered it, he would reward with a blow with his umbrella to the bike's rear mudguard.

Another bane of Eric's life in HK was the Chinese habit of spitting in public. To hear a Chinese spit is a never-to-be-forgotten experience. He/she seems to reach down to the soles of their feet before gurgitating with the most stomach-turning, retching sound. Then they dispose of the consequent deposit from this manoeuvre on to the pavement or wherever they happen to be. Whenever Eric was near a spitter (usually a man) he would upbraid him in no uncertain manner. After all, when the Japanese saw anyone spitting like that they were likely to have him executed.

I found it hilarious one morning while walking down Nathan Road on the way to work. A few yards ahead of me was another chap from the Mess, a fellow Scot. He was rapidly catching up with Eric. As he came within a few feet, he emitted the horrible Chinese spitting sound. Furious, Eric turned round with raised umbrella as if ready to strike the offender. However, no harm was done and a good laugh was had by all. I should say that Eric was an exception for, despite what appeared to be excessive behaviour in this regard, he was in fact a very decent individual with whom I was friendly during most of my three years' stay in HK. He as treasurer and I as secretary organised many fund-raising events for the residents and others - such as boat-trips, cocktail parties, Housey-Housey (Bingo). Takings from the bar helped to keep our Mess bills down and fund the expenses for the entertainment provided. The only time I spent out of the colony was when Eric and I went to Macao for a weekend. Quite an interesting place where one was just a few yards from Red Army Guards, on a bridge connecting to the mainland. Poor Eric died from a brain haemorrhage in his early thirties, as I learned a few years later while I was in Canada.

When Eric first arrived in HK he was given a party in his honour by his boss. Sadly, he over-indulged and ended up being sick in his boss's bedroom. He made a vow not to touch any alcoholic drink until he boarded the homeward-bound ship three years hence. Sure enough, on the appointed day he stood at the ship's guardrail with a glass to his lips, the first since his disastrous arrival.

It's strange, is it not, that such a friendly relationship as we had together and with others would, a few decades later, be regarded with suspicion.

There were other notable characters in the Mess, a couple of whom, namely Walter Webb and "Dolly" Gray, remain firmly in my memory for different reasons. Where Walter took no part in Mess life, even for meals, Dolly was a gregarious type and Mess Chairman. Walter, or Pau Tau as he was called by the Chinese because of his full head of almost white hair, was the dockyard Welfare Officer, responsible for the hiring and firing of Chinese employees, and as such had much influence in the community. I knew little of his background except that he had been born in Dalziel Place, Edinburgh. He was probably in his sixties in the early 1950s when I met him and had already been in HK for a number of years. I have little doubt that he carried on working and living in HK to the end.

Meantime Lieut. Dolly Gray (retd), who had been commissioned from the ranks quite late in his service, had the posh English accent cultivated as befitting his officer status. His job was to manage the safe-keeping of the various classified publications held within the Dockyard. A man of strict habits, one had a good idea of where he might be at any time of day.

After finishing work he would make his way to a certain café and spend an hour or two drinking gin. This in the company of prostitutes who would sit knitting sweaters or whatever while they chatted, joked or sang popular songs. Returning to the Mess, he would have another gin then retire to his room before returning for the evening meal. Finally at 9 p.m., after a couple of whiskies at the bar, he would retire to his room for the night. Only on special occasions would he change this behaviour. We corresponded for a few years.

Anyway, what was it that I was sent to HK to do? Well, I had a desk and filing cabinet and shared a large office with an English executive officer, a Chinese chief clerk called Mr. Ho and a dozen or so clerks, messengers and cleaners. In an adjoining office was the Secretary to the Commodore Superintendent. This Naval Commander was responsible for the Dockyard as well as being the Commander-in-Chief, Far East, and divided his time between this separately situated civilian office and the one staffed by the Navy personnel. Naturally, being an active dockyard concerned with the repair and modification to various types of warships, it was about these matters that The Secretary kept the CS informed.

Meanwhile, my role was minor, if varied. The main job I had was to arrange the booking of berths on the main ship (the *Chusan*) for those who had completed their tour. As said earlier, this was for 3 years for foremen and below unless accompanied by their wife. Once a month I'd visit the offices of Jardine-Matheson, the agents for P and O where Mr Stark and I spent a few hours on the complicated task of allocating berths according to rank, gender and age (family members). Apart from that and the testing of Chinese female applicants for secretary posts in dockyard departments, my memory fails me. I think I was more actively involved in Mess matters!

The *Chusan* was a new ship at the time of my going to HK. It was noted as being one of the first ships to be fitted with stabilisers to help combat the rolling action in rough weather. Nevertheless a period of 4 weeks at sea between HK and the UK seemed a very long time. But that was the only mode of conveyance available to us in those days. Nowadays, of course, the journey takes a matter of hours now that flying is so far advanced and has superseded seaborne travel.

Returning to HK 7 years after my first visit revealed a considerable number of contrasts. The most noticeable of these was the massive jump in population; there seemed to be just a few thousand in 1946, which by 1953 had topped 2 million and rising. The initial increase was caused by those who had escaped neutral Macau, many of them Portuguese/Chinese. Others took refuge in HK from the advancing Red Army, many industrialists from Shanghai. The arrival of the latter in the mid '50s ended the special treatment previously extended to British expats in hotels, restaurants etc.; it was the newcomers who had the money now!

Another change in the same vein was where before the War, and for a few years afterwards, business establishments accepted cheques from U.K. expatriates; this ended when a growing number of individuals abused the privilege with cheques that bounced.

Like all visitors, one had to take the trip on the Peak tram. This vehicle climbed by means of a system of powered ratchets and cables up to the top of the c1000 ft. hill from where, weather permitting, could be seen a vast panorama of islands, waterways and mainland, including Kowloon and the New Territories.

When I took a trip on the tram in '46, the buildings that lined the track on both sides, which were former residences of the elite, were ruins, the result of Japanese bombing 4 years earlier. Now, in '53, posh houses reaching to the summit had been built, with others lower down housing civil servants, nurses etc.

Nathan Road, the broad street reaching into the centre of Kowloon and beyond from the Star Ferry terminal, was now a busy thoroughfare with a cinema, restaurants and a large variety of shops, in contrast to the emptiness I had experienced previously. In fact the street could almost be compared with Princes Street, Edinburgh, the broad pavement on the shopping side being just as crowded.

When I was returning from work on one occasion and fighting my way through the milling throng on the aforesaid pavement (sidewalk) I came face to face with a young Chinese chap who barged into me. As he did so I felt a movement against my shirt pocket which held my quite expensive ball-point pen. Instinctively I grabbed him. But too late, my pen had gone – to his accomplice, no doubt. Breaking free, he ran off and although I tried to indicate my problem to the Chinese policemen directing traffic further on, there was of course, the language barrier. No great loss and a lesson learned even when, forty-five years later, I had my pocket picked in Istanbul. Again no great loss because I had only a few pounds in an old wallet while my good wallet which contained a good deal more money, plus credit cards and passport, I had left safely at daughter Sarah's.

Our Mess was in an old building situated on Austin Road which lay to the right at the summit of Nathan Road. It was close to a mile from the Star Ferry and we walked to and from the landing stage morning, lunchtime and after work five and a half days a week (this was before a 5-day week became mandatory). We'd then board a boat which chug-chugged us into the dockyard and our workplaces. Incidentally, I saw the actor Clark Gable a short distance from where we were boarding. (Must have been making one of his Chinese action films, usually corny.)

We were crossing the harbour on our return to work one lunchtime when there was a shout that someone was in the water a short distance away just as a Star ferry passed going the other way. Quickly, the crew headed towards him, a Chinese male, and tossed a lifebelt in his direction but out of his reach. Whereupon, without thinking, I jumped overboard, grabbed the belt and swam with it until it was within the man's reach. Members of the crew then pulled us to the boat by the line attached to the lifebelt, hauled us aboard and proceeded to pump water out of the man's lungs while he lay face down on the deck. Meanwhile my dockyard colleagues who had not raised a finger to help - because it was only a Chinese? –were silent, which made me feel like a twerp for what must have seemed to them an unnecessary display of heroics on my part. Be that as it may, the victim came to the Mess weeks later to thank me and left a silver cup as a reward. He was one of the Shanghaiese I mentioned earlier. I don't think I found out whether he fell, was pushed or jumped from the ferry. For me it had been no big deal; the water was warm, and I had swum a lot since coming to the colony. Also, I was wearing a shirt and shorts plus stockings and lightweight shoes which dried quickly in the hot sun.

There were a number of po-faced types in the Mess, ready to criticise, but slow to help or participate in, the various events held periodically, such as the celebration of the Queen's birthday, Burns Night (I think!), cocktail parties with senior dockyard managers, naval and civilian, and their wives invited and of course, Halloween, Christmas and New Year. It was ironic that once I introduced Housey-Housey (Bingo) with former Mess members and their wives added to their number, that even the staidest of these individuals participated; they made good use of the bar during the evening and on occasion became the most raucous.

The climate suited me fine with plenty of sunshine for most of the year, when dress was white shirt and shorts and white stockings during working hours. From January to March, though, it was cool enough for sports jacket and flannels and an open coal fire in the Mess. Unfortunately there is that time of year around September/October when humidity is extremely high. This makes sleeping difficult. Normal beds with mattresses are exchanged for camp-beds at this time – otherwise the former would be soaked in perspiration.

I was in my element here with plenty of sunshine and first-class beaches for swimming. One was Repulse Bay, which had three floating platforms, probably 100 yards offshore and the same distance between them. Swimming from one to the other in sea-water, the temperature of which made one want to stay there all day, was amazingly comfortable. Trouble was that because this beach was so accessible it got very busy at times.

It was on Sundays that we'd hire a crewed boat from the dockyard, stock it with cases of beer, soft drinks and sandwiches and along with former Mess members, their wives and children, head out for Clearwater Bay. I think it was about an hour's run, with sharks appearing now and then when their dorsal fins broke the surface.

The beach was accessible only by sea and usually deserted. The water was just as the name describes it, clear – so much so that though the bottom was at a depth that caused eardrums to crinkle when diving down to it, the sandy bottom could be seen from the surface with amazing clarity.

I'm describing this beach as it was about 60 years ago i.e. 1953-'56. Now, I understand, a road has been built to it and it is thronged with day trippers from the city (Victoria) and elsewhere. Such is progress!

For a while I made use of the 50 metre open-air pool in the dockyard during my lunch-hour. If there were more than three sailors there at one time it was busy.

Apart from the people I mentioned earlier there were many others I had close association with. My boss, the Secretary to the Commodore Superintendent, was Henry Ball, a gregarious type in his early fifties who had played football as an English Schools' Internationalist. We got on well together both at the workplace and socially. He wanted me to stay over my time and replace the Executive Officer who was due to end his tour and return to the UK a month after me. However, despite this offer of promotion I felt that a three-year tour without a home leave had been overlong in itself. I had had enough of the place. The Executive Officer and I just tolerated each other, he being a tall English type with the slightly superior manners adopted by those risen from humble backgrounds and usually from the London area. In winter he'd wear a sports jacket with sleeves too short and grey flannels at half-mast. Also, he used a purse for his money. He probably thought me a bit too independent and dismissive of his rank, which of course I was. And this was a trait I carried throughout my future career, perhaps!

Most of my social life was centred on the Mess events, visits to the cinema and restaurants and various beaches. At first I was accompanied by Mac and Steve, mainly the former, for at forty Steve seemed old. However, with a wife and family in the UK he was more responsible than his tearaway companions who made the most of a single man's freedom in this exciting place. Later I kept company with a typist from the engineering department whose knowledge of HK added interest. Patsy was a twenty-one-year-old Portuguese/Chinese whose mother had died, leaving her father and a teenage brother and sister. The father was a major-domo in the Peninsula Hotel, Kowloon and they lived in company property next to the hotel.

Sadly, the father too died and under embarrassing circumstances. He had a heart-attack while at an inn in the company of an elderly neighbour's much younger wife. Consequently Patsy and her brother and sister had to leave the hotel's premises and move into a flat near the Kai Tak airport.

I enjoyed Pat's company to the point where marriage was hinted at but I am afraid my feelings towards her Roman Catholicism were and still are so antagonistic that I didn't feel such a union would work. The thought that any offspring would have to be brought up as Catholics, while a priest would come round visiting etc., gave me cold feet. As it happens, she got married to another chap, an English executive officer in the Engineer's Department, as I saw in the South China Morning Post the day before I sailed for home.

I liked and admired the Chinese, especially those like Mr. Ho, the chief clerk, who like many others had spent the War in Macau and Tang, who managed the Mess. It would be interesting to return to see how the former colony is under Beijing's control. But that is highly unlikely now.

A farewell gathering of Commodore Superintendent & HK dockyard office staff for the return to the UK of Seaborne & myself.

The farewell dinner

Chatting with Commodore Thorold C-in-C Far East Fleet

Former telegraph boys – self, Reverend Jimmy Monaghan, padre of Royal Scots battalion New Territories, and John Pollock, executive officer dockyard cash office.

The dockyard cricket team

So on February 1, '56 I waved goodbye to HK and headed home and to a job at my former dockyard - Rosyth. The voyage home was an anti-climax. Three years before, I had sailed on the *Chusan* full of eager anticipation and though, as I've mentioned, the time there without a break seemed overlong, it was an experience I would have hated to miss. I had no such anticipation for my return to Rosyth, but of course I was keen to see my family, who had moved from Niddrie Mains to the Inch in '51.

On arriving at Tilbury and in the Customs shed, I was pleasantly surprised by wee sister Jean, now an elegant young lady of 23, who had travelled down from Edinburgh to meet me. This was quite a tonic in view of the fact that the Customs Officer checking my luggage was a horror who humiliated me unnecessarily, suggesting a strip search because I had forgotten to declare the wrist-watch I'd got the year before. This didn't happen but he did charge me for every item I had declared.

The '56 winter had been very severe with lots of snow over the UK and Europe. The *Chusan* had called in at Marseilles and even here, on the Med., there had been snow. Yet within a couple of days of arriving home I was playing on Prestonfield golf-course in my shirt-sleeves.

The Rosyth job was another wash-out. I sat at a large desk with a young chap facing me and with two young girls, one at each end. It may have been good fun at times but not worth the effort of travelling to and from home. I can't remember what I was supposed to be doing but it certainly wasn't a lot. At one point I was sent to Admiralty, London, for an interview for promotion to executive officer. Sitting facing five or six suits across a long desk, I answered questions put to me reasonably well, I think, but when asked how working in Admiralty compared with the Post Office I said how I found the tempo of the former much slower. I did not succeed.

By this time, however, I was considering a move to Canada. This was the result of Joan Riley, the typist in the HK office, saying how she and her husband Bill and the children would be leaving to join her parents in Vancouver Island and that I too should "go West, young man!". Her father had been a HK policeman gaoled by the Japanese. By coincidence a woman clerk in the Secretary to the Admiral's office, Jean Cummings, was about to join her husband in Toronto and offered me accommodation there. So, when Ann convinced me in September of that year (1956) that this seemed a good idea and also confirmed a desire to go with me, this is what happened the following May.

My first ever visit to Skye, where Ann grew up, had taken place in September, '56 when, with Ann, I went by train via Inverness to Kyle, then by ferry to Kyleakin. It being 1956, Ann stayed overnight at Kyle View with her Auntie Maggie while I dossed down at Rona Cottage. Poor old Maggie had her reservations about me, the more so when she learned of my intention to whisk her niece off to Canada, leaving her Mother behind.

Marrying on the 6th, we sailed from Liverpool to Montreal on the 8th aboard the *Saxonia*.

We docked in Montreal after a week's voyage which, despite the occasion, was quite uneventful. We transferred to a train bound for Toronto in the company of many others from Europe hoping for a new life with great expectations. I was sorry for the young German in our compartment, a carpenter whose carefully made trunk holding the precious tools of his trade had been mercilessly hacked open by Customs because he had mislaid his key for opening it. A decided lack of sensitivity and not a good omen for a newcomer to the country. Anyway, we were met at the railway station by the Cummings, who drove us to their home in Scarborough, a Toronto suburb, where we stayed for about a week.

Ann and I were somewhat apprehensive in this new situation. We appreciated our good fortune in having a place to put down our heads but were anxious at the same time to get out on our own. We were lucky, for this didn't take long – something like two weeks.

I had seen an ad in the paper for a payroll clerk and on phoning I was invited to attend for an interview. The company was Regent Oil, a British-owned refinery on the shores of Lake Ontario at Port Credit, another Toronto suburb but at the other end of the city, ie to the west. I was interviewed by a manager, Joe Lailey, an Englishman, and given the job.

I had mixed feelings about this as I'd hoped to enter a completely different career, having left the Civil Service and, hopefully, the clerical type of work I'd been accustomed to. However, this job would give us a toehold and the opportunity to establish ourselves quickly and independently.

Having accepted the offer of the job, ie making up the salaries of tanker and truck drivers, we had to find a suitable place to stay. Here again, we were lucky, there being 1-bedroom flats available in a newly-built development at Longbranch, again at Lake Ontario, about 2 miles from the refinery.

Once we had moved into the flat and I had started work, Ann thought she'd look for a job.

Well, she was a brave soul; first she worked in a laundry, ironing; then waited with other immigrants of all nationalities for a pick-up truck to take them to the fields to pick strawberries; then she walked for miles within the district selling educational books; all this at the height of summer. Meanwhile she had successfully applied for an English-teacher vacancy in Etobicoke, Toronto, not realising that she was pregnant with Moira; so she withdrew. From then until we left for Pembroke the following June she helped look after kids in a mobile home parked permanently across the street – as well as – but not together with, her own kid when she arrived in March.

There were two of us in the payroll office, plus a part-time woman. My boss Don was a young conscientious chap with a wife and a youngster. A nice Canadian family still in the process of building their own house out in the country. We were invited there for a meal at Thanksgiving – or was it Christmas?

*Ann's parents,
Mr and Mrs Macdiarmid*

When later I resigned from the company, which became owned by Texaco and located in Bloor Street, opposite the University Stadium in downtown Toronto, I felt a sense of guilt at leaving Don after such a short spell.

Moira arrived in '58 and soon afterwards we moved to Pembroke, Ontario, where I had secured a job with the Eddy Match Company. My boss was an Englishman, Ken Eperon, who had interviewed me in Toronto. He had the task of processing the backlog of orders which had accumulated following the transfer of the company from Hull, Quebec, some months previously and he needed assistance with this. It was a question of liaising with the customer for his requirements as expressed by sales, with the supplier of printing plates specific for the order and with the factory staff who scheduled production and manufacture and shipping of the order within a specified period. We're talking Advertising Bookmatches where the customer submitted his design for the cover, colours etc. It was a very competitive market, especially when the Japanese came into it.

When Ken left the company a few years later I took over from him until I was asked if I'd take over the job of cost accountant, the incumbent having been fired because he'd failed to cope with the newly introduced job-costing system after 3 months at it. I accepted the same day, a Friday, and was at my new desk inside the factory next day – and what a shambles there was – paper tapes from adding machines piled high from my predecessor's attempts to balance figures. However, working alongside Chief Accountant Rick Moore, I managed to issue a monthly document detailing the costs of each job produced, with comments, and to show the actual costs of material and labour against standard (predetermined) costs.

We had been very fortunate in getting accommodation over the seven years of our stay. At first we lodged with the Cummings, then were the first entrants to a rented flat in a new block situated close to Lake Ontario in the Toronto suburb of Longbranch in the two or three weeks following our arrival in the country. The flat was unfurnished except for a cooker. There was a laundry downstairs for general use and I suppose we must have got the bed, chairs, etc. on the never-never. Anyway, we were there for just about a year when we moved north two hundred miles to Pembroke and my new job.

For a few months we rented a long-established apartment in the centre of town, until we moved to the new detached bungalow which was our home till we returned to Scotland six years later. We had managed to buy it under a mortgage scheme operated by the Ontario Government. It was still being built while we were in the apartment in town and we couldn't wait for it to be completed. So between May '57 when we left the ship and August '58 we were fortunate to be able to buy our own home.

The house was in a subdivision about five miles from Pembroke, with a fairly small number of other homes, well separated, above a wooded slope overlooking the Ottawa River and Quebec on the other side. It became quite a close-knit community. Ann and other wives would meet for evenings of Canasta while the men gathered in front of the TV to watch ice-hockey and drink bottles of cold beer.

Moira, born in Toronto and only 18 months when we moved in, had many playmates about the same age. It was only later that a problem arose - there was no suitable school nearby.

It was a great environment for adults and children. Summers were hot but not oppressive, except for mosquitoes, while winters were more than a little chilly but with clear blue skies and bright landscapes. One of the most spectacular sights one could imagine was the night sky, with the stars so close above one's head, especially since we had no street-lights. We actually saw Russia's Sputnik as it made its way around the Earth - just like a brilliant star moving laterally. And this with the naked eye.

There was one winter when I went out to our car, a Mini, and found the temperature at -40°F. Fortunately I had a block heater attached to an outside electrical wall socket. The Mini started, but when it began to move there were loud noises from the frozen lubricants in the wheel bearings. Nevertheless I got to work with the help of two passengers, neighbours and colleagues whose large American cars failed to cope with the low temperature. My passengers had to keep clearing the windscreen during the journey to town, the Mini's heater proving ineffective.

The fact that we were living in a hunting/shooting/fishing area was confirmed a few times. While readying for work one morning I looked out from the kitchen window to see a large black bear rummaging in our garbage can. Another morning I nearly caught up with a large moose padding down the highway in front of me before disappearing into the undergrowth. It was not unusual to hear wolves howling at night - fortunately in the distance.

I became a member of the local Royal Canadian Air Force Association and was soon talked into being treasurer. It was as such that at our annual Stepdancing and Fiddling Contest I had the role of collecting the entrance money. At the end of the evening, after having written cheques for the prize winners, another member and I took the takings to the bank, where he was assistant manager, for safekeeping overnight. Next morning, a Sunday, a neighbour who came to our door and asked for me must have had thoughts when Moira, who answered, told him that I was at the bank counting my money. I was at the bank certainly, but it was not my money of course.

In '63 it was decided that the President and executives of Eddie Match would be relocated in Toronto; I moved back into the office to learn the financial accounting side of the business, with a view to taking over when the others had departed. Unfortunately, I found this aspect of accounting boring and was unable to enjoy it. Then, when I asked for a week's unpaid leave to add to the fortnight I was due so that my first visit home to Scotland for seven years would really be worth the effort, Rick refused me. This hurt because I had given many hours of overtime during the early days without compensation in payment or time off.

So, with Ann's worries about her mother's health and living conditions in my mind and the drawback of not having a suitable school for Moira in the area on top of my problems, it was decided to sell up and return to Scotland, which we did on board ship (*The Empress of Canada*) from Montreal in June, '64. So farewell to Canada, but not forever.

The big day!!

On the way to Canada

Ann at Niagara Falls, our honeymoon location

Moira in the snow

After seven years away, the material gains of the Scots stood out. Many more people had cars, telephones, refrigerators, washing machines and TVs than ever before. The never-never was now in full swing, which enabled people to have these things. Now supermarkets were appearing, to the dismay of the small shopkeepers who could not match the variety of goods on sale or the lower prices offered, achieved through mass purchasing.

Although jobs were plentiful because of a period of full employment, they were inclined to be the more menial ones in factories, etc. I hoped to get a position equivalent to or better than the one I'd left. I had a sealed letter of recommendation from the Factory Director of Eddy Match addressed to a friend of his in a management consultancy in London but didn't follow this through. However, my application to McVitie & Price resulted in the offer of a job entitled Factory Efficiency Manager – the best of all the jobs I ever had, anywhere. I reported to the Assistant Factory Director, Dougal Reid, former Watsonian and Black Watch Officer in Burma during the War (1939-45). I had the run of the factory and with a number of recommendations saved the company £100,000 or so during the 2 years I was there. In '66 the factory closed and I transferred to Macfarlane-Lang in Glasgow, now also part of the United Biscuits group.

This move was an upheaval for the family. We had bought a house in Oxgangs Road, Edinburgh after giving up the bungalow we'd rented in Eskbank. Ann had taught in the Primary School in Bonnyrigg, while 6-year-old Moira attended Dalkeith Primary. Mrs. Macdiarmid had been living with us in the bungalow but had left for Edinbane, Skye. She passed away there, in Edinbane, in August, '65.

Now faced with my transfer to Glasgow, we felt we had to locate somewhere near to the factory and chose Lenzie. This was sad because it meant our leaving Edinburgh. Also it was another change of school for Moira, who had gone from Dalkeith Primary to Morningside Primary, and on to the elitist Mary Erskine. Now she was to experience the limitations of a school in Lenzie which lacked regular teaching staff. Fortunately she was able to rise above this failing as the future showed. Meanwhile Ann was pregnant with Sarah, who arrived within a few months of our move.

Our new house, a Miller home, was quite good, situated as it was in a quiet residential area with pleasant neighbours. Unfortunately, though, my experience at Macfarlane-Lang was miserable, mainly because of my successes at the factory I'd just left. To explain, my former Factory Director visited and lauded me to his counterpart, to whom I now reported. However, one individual who had been an Assistant Production Manager at McVitie's and had also transferred, put it about that the figures I'd been using to achieve my results were faked. It was obvious to me that this was an attempt to cover up for the shortcomings I'd explored in his performances in Edinburgh. Unfortunately, because I was relatively new to the Company, and, of course, to the technicalities of baking biscuits, he was believed.

I was given a different job here so that I could learn more of the business. I was now a Shift Manager. This meant that I was responsible for the factory's operation outside the normal hours, when fewer biscuit ovens were in use, ie 2 pm to 10 pm.

The usual biscuits being made were Digestive, Rich Tea, Chocolate Digestive, Bunty Sponge, Ginger Nuts and Custard Creams. It was with Digestives that I had my biggest fracas.

One afternoon at the start of my evening shift, the Factory Director instructed me to make sure that an urgent Sales demand for Chocolate Digestives was completed. Unfortunately, it being a warm summer's evening, there was difficulty with the chocolate – it was still soft on the biscuits when they reached the wrapping machines. To try to overcome this I instructed the ovensman to slow the conveyor belt carrying the biscuits to the chocolate enrober, thus reducing their temperature and hopefully, with the additional drop in temperature as they went through the cooling tunnels, making it possible for them to be wrapped - and it worked - until instructions were given to stop by the foreman in charge of chocolate production. I, in turn, countermanded his order and the biscuits continued to be produced.

Next day, the Asst. Factory Director, a chocolate specialist, gave me a dressing-down for telling his foreman what to do. I didn't say much in response but contributed to his being made redundant a few months later. The thing was that the system was wrong, as was later recognised. Only one person should have had control of the operation from beginning to end, which is how I saw it.

The next problem was with Plain Digestive, the former Asst. Production Manager from Edinburgh had run the oven band so fast that the biscuits weren't properly baked and because of breakages the wrapping girls couldn't use the wrapping machines and instead picked the biscuits off the bands and stacked them in tins. He had gone home when I took over, leaving a note not to bake any more biscuits until all those in tins had been cleared.

This made me see red, because our performance was judged to a great extent by the amount of waste biscuit produced on one's shift and it was obvious that I would inherit much more than I deserved because of his failure. Unfortunately my objections were disregarded and I was the one made to feel as though I should have done as he had instructed, in the eyes of the Factory Director who had, no doubt, been given a coloured version of the event.

So, generally speaking, I didn't feel at all welcome here and was only too pleased when Dougal Reid invited me to join him at HQ in Osterley, West London. So it was up sticks and away again!

From March to June '68 I commuted to London weekly by train (1st class sleeper on Sunday night), returning by air to Glasgow on Friday evening. During the week I stayed in a hotel not far from Heathrow and close to Southall where Auntie Peggy and Uncle Andrew Dryburgh with cousin Elizabeth had lived before emigrating to New Zealand in '54.

I would arrive at Euston Station about 6 am and make my way to the office at Osterley I shared with Dougal. Invariably he would be at his desk when I arrived, for it was the practice of the MD (Hector Laing) and his senior staff to be on the premises around 7 am and to have breakfast together at 8 am. I had mine with the junior managers in a separate dining-room at the same time.

I now had a new title – Production Services Admin. Manager. Briefly, the job was to assist Dougal in monitoring the production performances of the five biscuit factories that made up United Biscuits at that time and to confirm the standards set for the input of each biscuit line against actual output of product. This served at least two purposes, the first to measure production efficiency, the second to provide Sales & Marketing with the figures needed to make forecasts for the following year with regard to quantities and costs. I designed a standard form which each factory used to advise us of the elements of production each month. I analysed these and made appropriate comments, which I distributed to the senior managers in HQ and to the Factory Directors. Once a year I accompanied Dougal to each factory where he negotiated biscuit production standards for the following year. I enjoyed the privilege of flying 1st Class to Manchester, Liverpool and Glasgow with Dougal, but this was only because I was with him – otherwise I flew tourist class. There were other aspects of the job I enjoyed, but mainly the favourable recognition I received from group senior staff for Accounting and Production. I was called upon to make presentations concerning certain aspects of the factories' performances, based on the figures I'd gathered and analysed, on a number of occasions. This gave me some job satisfaction. Sadly, this was not to last. Before continuing, however, I feel that I should deal with our domestic circumstances at this time.

During the months while I was commuting, I spent time house-hunting and found what became our home for 17 years in Maidenhead, Berks. A detached house with 3 bedrooms, kitchen, lounge/dining-room, workshop, bathroom, separate toilet and a nice garden. Home for Moira and Sarah until they left for University some years later.

For me, living so far away from my place of work was a bit of a bind, especially when the left-hand-drive Morris 1100 we'd brought over on the ship from Canada turned out to be a rust-bucket and in need of replacement. Still, I think I will leave my experience with cars alone – it was unfortunate to say the least until we were in the position of being able to buy a new one.

Ann's time for the first few years was taken up looking after Sarah, who was only 13 months when we moved to Maidenhead. Later she taught English at various schools in the area until 1985 when we retired to Skye.

Over the years we had visits from Grandma & Grandad Danskin who would stay for a couple of weeks or so. They very much enjoyed the warmer temperatures and the garden. We also had other relatives and various friends of the girls, French and German, staying at various times. It was a useful place from which to tour historic features, including those in London, of course.

On one occasion I took relatives with me into Westminster Abbey. I wanted them to see the Stone of Scone which I'd seen on previous visits. This time there was no sign of it. I queried the uniformed official at the exit, who replied, "I'm not telling you where it is. You're a Scotsman!". It seems that for some reason the cabinet it rested in was closed on Sundays. Now, of course, it's safely back in Scotland.

Except for Moira, who left for Bath University on reaching 18, we lived in the house for 17 years before making, for Ann and me, our final move. Sarah entered Edinburgh University the same year. Meanwhile I reached a turning point in my career. I went downward.

It came about when the Group Production Director died and was replaced by the Factory Director of the Harlesden Factory, a certain John Finlayson. This was the job Dougal Reid had aspired to, but instead he was switched to the vacancy at Harlesden – with a colour TV as part compensation. So I had a new boss.

Without going into detail, we were not compatible and he decided that he no longer wanted me as his aide. It was then that I made a wrong decision which I'm sure blighted the remainder of my working life. In my job monitoring factories production, I worked in close liaison with the Group Cost Accountant, but when it was put to me that I should work for him I didn't give myself sufficient time to consider. Instead I turned down the offer more or less without thinking – but why? Well, I felt that in the job I was leaving I had equal status with the Cost Accountant, yet at the same time I felt that my lack of formal accounting qualifications would count against me. However, pulling for me was the Group Financial Director, who had interviewed me when I first applied for the Edinburgh job. He and Dougal were good friends. My only consolation is that I may not have made the grade anyway and that the years ahead provided variety if not prosperity.

After a few months doing a piddling job with a chap responsible for packaging, I foolishly accepted a transfer to Harlesden, not to work directly with my former boss, but with an idle character who had the job I had pioneered at Robertson Ave. This was a come-down, of course, but it was a job at a time when both girls were at school, Sarah having just started and Moira only 14. As it happened, I managed to free myself from my new boss and set about revamping the Stores, a vast area beneath the cake bakehouse containing some £1 million worth of mechanical and electrical parts for use on the biscuit and cake ovens in this 24/7 factory, the largest in Europe.

The parts were located in metal bins resting on shelves on Dexion racks which in turn rested almost completely on the concrete floors. Consequently the place was overrun by mice, there being no access under the racks for cleaning and there were many of them. Also the procedures for ordering parts were quite chaotic and in need of revision. I had two predecessors who had advanced so far with their ideas for improvement, then given up and disappeared. First was an Army Brigadier (retd.) followed by an RAF Wing Commander who had been in charge of Far East logistics – or so I was told.

With the aid of the Chief Engineer, who provided me with a couple of labourers and a deaf-mute typist (the result of measles?), I spent about 18 months sorting the place out.

We started by demolishing the racks one by one, recording the items contained in the bins and allocating each its own computerised number which I listed under type headings. The racks were then reassembled with the lower shelf a foot or so off the floor to allow for easy access. It was hot working beneath the cake ovens and under fluorescent lighting all the time – and this was from about 7.15 am until after 4, although nobody checked my hours. It meant an early start, leaving home at 6.15 and driving on the M4, then up to Harlesden in North London. I must have been mad!

Still, completing this job gave me some satisfaction. I introduced the system where the clerk receiving stores used a gun on which he entered the computer number of items on to labels which, when stuck on, identified them for storage, extraction and issuing.

I suggested that a hair-dryer should be used to shrink-wrap cases of biscuits when there were not enough of them to be wrapped in the usual shrink-wrapping machine. Soon there were hair-dryers in use night and day. Although I had allocated each part a computer number and Headquarters were keen to develop this into the Group's computer system, I did not feel that at that time computers were at a suitable stage for this. I'd say that another 20 years or so were to elapse before they were suitable. For even in 1980 when I ran into a similar situation at GEC (explained later) the present level of computer usage was still a few years away.

Once the revamped stores were up and running, I was asked to investigate weaknesses in the operations for maintaining supplies of baking and wrapping materials over the 24/7 production of biscuits and cakes. There were one or two significant tasks I came upon which needed to be changed for improved efficiency. Following this I was offered the job about to be vacated by the incumbent manager whose responsibility it was to ensure that there was no breakdown in the production of any line through a shortage of materials. A very large responsibility indeed, when losses of product and wasted labour hours occur should the ovens come to a halt and staff be sent home. It seemed to me obvious that to do the job effectively I would need to be on call in case of emergencies arising because of such shortcomings and that living out at Maidenhead made this out of the question. I certainly had no wish to move house to be nearer the factory so I turned down the offer and after a few enquiries I returned to HQ, Osterley.

Here I joined the Personnel or, as it is now, Human Resources Department. When I encountered the Financial Director and his assistant soon after my arrival, they guffawed at my latest move and rightly so.

My work was varied and interesting only because of the freedom I had to more or less do my own thing. There was routine which kept me in the office, such as summarising statistics relating to hours employed at the factories and working out redundancy payments etc. However, periodically I joined with a female Personnel Manager to represent management and, along with two Trade Union reps, visit factories on job-evaluation exercises. We'd be away for a few days, staying overnight in hotels.

Talking of hotels reminds me of the set-up I introduced whereby UB salesmen and others could get low rates at those places I had visited around the country and negotiated with. I produced a card listing the hotels and their agreed tariffs, which the travellers could carry with them.

Commuting to Osterley by car was much easier than the drive to Harlesden, of course, being much nearer. My working hours and physical conditions were also much improved. Nevertheless I was not satisfied with my lot and applied for other jobs outside of UB. One source I contacted sent on an abbreviated version of my CV to about 50 companies. In due course I received a positive response.

The job was as Administrative Manager with GEC Overseas Services whose office was near The Strand and Drury Lane. The company as part of GEC was in two parts, one of which installed lighting in arenas etc. at home and overseas. The other, where I was employed, was concerned mainly with airfield lights, also at home and abroad. It seems that the MD was attracted to me by my Stores experience along with that of Accounting. The stores at Harlesden may have been chaotic but they were nothing compared with what I was faced with here. Whereas the parts in the Biscuit Factory were for usage internally, here they were sent out to customers or to Company projects at various airfields, five of which were in Nigeria.

The Stores were held in two places, the glass for lamps at a private warehouse up in Newcastle and electrical and mechanical parts in a shared building in Rotherham, East London. Recording of transactions was carried out in the office, with information supplied through paper-work – orders, invoices etc. raised there and by the Stores Manager in Rotherham. Only he knew what he had stored there and was able to identify the items. And this was no easy task because many items had been modified to meet customers' requirements, some over and over again, so much so that the original description was meaningless when it came to ordering.

Those responsible in the office for recording the movement of stock had such a crazy set-up that it was next to incomprehensible. The personnel here were ancient and happily soldiering on until all were cleared out within a few months of my arrival.

Although Accounting was supposedly part of my duties, this was a misnomer, for that function was the responsibility of two qualified accountants who managed the finances of both parts of the company. For a while I authorised expenses of those in the office and provided the accountants with various monthly returns, the purpose of which I can't remember.

Once the deadwood was removed from that part of the office concerned with stock control, I was left with a staff of 6 men. I'm still not clear what the duties of two of them were! I had a young German chap who'd applied for a job with me but on looking around the main office, said "This is pre-war!" and left. And how right he was.

The furniture was very pre-1939, having been transferred from the original GEC building, now occupied by the Civil Air Authority (CAA). Some chairs had long lost their upholstery and in one case a leg. This was the seat for a retired engineer whose expertise was such that he'd been retained far past his retirement date. Fortunately he worked part-time, which reduced the time he had to suffer. I made strong applications to my boss for a number of new chairs, but it took many months to get a half-dozen. The thing was that the company, the other half in particular, had lost a lot of money on contracts, so we all suffered. Besides, my boss and other Directors had no problem with flying on overseas trips. They went 1st class. Without my knowledge it was decided that the Stores in Rotherham should be transferred to premises in Barking. The storekeeper was to organise the move but would only agree to do so at a price – an increase in salary. When my boss disputed having agreed to the increase mentioned, the storekeeper took the matter to an Industrial Tribunal and lost. The consequence was that since the storekeeper had resigned it was left to me to take control of the move to Barking.

Fortunately I gained the help of two storemen from the new company, and between us we moved all the items to newly-built racks. This took time, of course, and much travel to and from the office on my part with the use of an old company car, or, from home, by train and the Underground. During the changeover orders were delayed, of course.. Also, the new storemen were unfamiliar with the items asked for and I wasn't much better. So at some point I repeated what I had done in the Harlesden stores by giving each item its own computer number. Also I designed a new set of 6-page forms, each page with its own colour, to identify it for order, shipping and invoicing, filing etc. Typed or written data went through on to each page without the need for messy carbons.

Numbering parts proved to be a bonus on my last visit to Nigeria. Over time the engineers at the five airfields under construction would ask for a part or parts to be sent out because previous requests for them had not arrived, although it was known at Head Office, London, that they had definitely been sent. Some, of course, were filched from the cases lying awaiting collection at Lagos Docks. There was the amusing instance when a Nigerian girl tried to sell what were obviously GEC's property to the storekeeper at the Lagos airfield.

I think one of the problems was the misinterpretation of the parts' description, with the result that the wrong item was received. Meanwhile this part was put aside to gather dust at one airfield while another airfield which had a need for it sent an order to London for the same item.

I visited Nigeria on three occasions between June 1980 and March 1981. On the first one I flew to four of the five airfields when the Company was installing airfield lighting on the runways and approaches. Working with the expatriate engineer at each, I recorded the amount of cable laid in order to confirm the amount claimed for by the consultants working on behalf of the Nigerian Air Authority. It was hot work trailing around behind a measuring wheel, made easier, though, when someone was able to hold it out of the door of a pick-up for the long runway measurements. It could prove hazardous when checking the transformer pits dotted the length of the runway. This was because it was sometimes difficult to distinguish a snake from the cable inside until, having been disturbed, the spitting cobra raised its head and spat at the disturber's eyes. This happened to one of the native labourers in our group at Port Harcourt Airfield. His mates rushed him quickly to a nearby village for treatment by the resident witch-doctor and I heard later that he was OK.

It was at Port Harcourt that I experienced the most frightening hours of my life when I was delayed from flying back to Lagos by an electrical storm. Having obtained a boarding-pass at a cost – a victim of corruption as normal in Nigeria – I waited along with a Sikh Professor from the local university, in the early afternoon. He was joining the same flight before carrying on to India. It was not until 10 pm that it was confirmed that the flight was cancelled because of the weather.

I was in a dilemma. Not enough money left, about 14 naira for a sandwich even if one had been available, never mind having enough for a hotel – no credit-card facilities then. So it was much to my relief that my professor companion said how he had friends with a small hotel in the city and that I would be welcome to go with him there despite my poverty.

Then who should arrive but the company driver with his pick-up, come to see how things were with me. He knew the locality of the hotel, so with great relief and gratitude we boarded the pick-up, unaware of the drama about to come.

As we travelled along the right half of an 8-lane highway divided into 4 lanes, each with a high central reservation broken at intervals, for emergencies, I think, our driver suddenly entered one of these breaks and turned right, thus facing the oncoming traffic. This as I learned later was because the hotel lay obliquely opposite – otherwise he'd have had to travel considerably further before turning back to join the opposite lanes. It seemed fortunate that only a few cars were on the road and on the other lanes, except for one which came towards us with headlights full on. Both vehicles came to a halt bonnet to bonnet, only a few feet apart. Then, out of the facing car came 6 or 7 men, taxi-drivers as it turned out, who raged at our driver and at `Whitey`, as they called me, for allowing our driver to enter the wrong lanes. So it was with some alarm I said to my Sikh friend, who had just pointed out the hotel to me: "Let's go!" and we did. Not very heroic, perhaps, but it did seem the best thing to do, as it turned out, despite the arrival of the police to disperse the gathering crowd. As I witnessed from the hotel, all was soon quiet. Nevertheless I lay awake most of the night in fear of the arrival of the police, knowing their reputation. However, at 6 o'clock or so in the morning we went by taxi to the airport. Only once airborne did I breathe a sigh of relief.

Sad to say, I didn't get the Professor's name or address to compensate him for his kindness. The Company driver was a tough cookie, a former sergeant with the Biafran army, and not one to take any nonsense. He came to the airport to see me off, none the worse for the previous night's encounter, it seemed.

On my return from my last visit to Nigeria, in March 1981, I learned that the Company was transferring to join up with another GEC Company at Rugby. I chose redundancy rather than continue working with a boss and others (all Welshmen) for whom I had lost confidence and respect. They were all for looking after themselves – first-class air travel etc. – yet pleading Company poverty when employing engineers to manage the Nigerian airfield contracts. It seemed that anyone who could hold a screwdriver would fill the bill and would be paid accordingly. Much delay and wastage resulted. So it was this lack of direction that caused the change of policy as ordered by Arnold Weinstock, who said that he could earn more from a Post Office bank account than from our Company. Not that he was to be admired for having taken over many Companies, with resultant redundancies. He used the vast wealth gathered as a fiscal weapon to build it further, to the neglect of his employees and their welfare. As an example, where other Companies such as United Biscuits would pay double the redundancy pay laid down by the Government, plus a figure for each year with the Company, GEC paid only the legal amount due. Also, as mentioned previously, the condition of offices such as ours would have been considered below par before the Second World War.

When Weinstock retired from the Chairmanship of GEC he was replaced by a former wonder-boy from BEA, who succeeded in running the whole caboodle into the ground when he decided to concentrate solely on Electronics. The Company never recovered from the losses incurred following the world-wide collapse of the electronics market during the end of the 1900s and the beginning of the new century. Now GEC no longer exists, having been appropriated by a Dutch Company - Plessey, I think.

Fortunately my pension was secured by some arrangement, not Plessey, which I was relieved to learn – but I'm not sure how it works.

Although I was prepared for redundancy, I did consider the options offered to me. One was to work in the Finance Dept. at HQ in Central London – Stanhope Gate - or at an office in Wembley, where I would take over from a retiree whose job was to look after GEC properties throughout the country and, as a sideline, provide the welfare arrangements for the nearby Company Club.

Meanwhile, having replied to an advert in The Observer calling for applicants for Middlesex Polytechnic (now University) to study for a degree course and been accepted following an interview at the Enfield site, I was left with a difficult decision. Frankly, I no longer had a taste for continuing with GEC when both jobs would have meant the usual commuting, although in the case of Wembley, moving house seemed the appropriate thing to do because of the Club connection.

As for the Polytechnic, it was a case of the need of support from the family because of my being away from home for much of the time over the 3-4 years of the course. Anyway, Ann and the girls seemed enthusiastic and unanimous in their feeling that I should have the chance to go to University – and this is what I did, starting in October '81 and graduating in June '85.

To have commuted daily to Enfield from Maidenhead would have been impractical, so I applied for accommodation to the Polytechnic office where lists were held and finished up with a retired couple in Enfield. I was with them for the few months until Xmas. They were a nice pair, a bit old-fashioned in their ways, but they did their best to make me feel comfortable. Sadly, I was the naughty one, for despite knowing that himself disliked it, I smoked my pipe in my room while studying. If only I could go back! I wasn't restricted with this bad habit from then onwards.

My second accommodation was a room in a block on the campus, which was pretty good. It was close to the Mess (Students' Union) on one side, and backed on to a forest. On occasions I would walk or jog along the path which bisected the forest, then come back another way. Despite my advanced years – 58/9 – I had no trouble mixing in with the other students, average age 27/8 for those on my course. I avoided the Union on the nights when live music was being belted out – a different era.

Otherwise, it was get-togethers over cups of coffee, chatting, discussing, arguing the pros and cons of the course, the lecturers, politics etc. I had a run-in with a very left-wing lecturer who resented my butting-in to a group he'd held back for further discussion following a lecture. They were an amalgam of Trotskyists, Marxist-Leninists, Maoists and whatever other types of that ilk there were. Because I had the audacity (ignorance?) to challenge some of their assertions, I was given my marching orders by the lecturer. Reporting this to my course leader evoked some mild sympathy, but nothing further – he, too, was a bit of a lefty. Of course I should have taken the hint and left with the others at the end of the lecture.

With colleagues at Middlesex University Trent Park near Enfield, 1981 - 1985

When my term in Halls came to an end I moved in with another student who had a house near Epping Forest. A nice chap but with a cleanliness phobia. He washed his hands constantly and even litter distressed him. I saw him pick up a matchstick from the beach on a field-trip to Devon, to dispose of it later. When his girlfriend, also on the course, moved in, I decided to move out. They married later.

At this time Moira and I exchanged visits, her digs being close to the Arsenal Football Ground.

What might seem a young man's dream was the make-up of my next place. It was a terraced house in Palmer's Green occupied by four young women of various occupations. However, as an old married man, I found it rather mundane. After all, I had my studies to attend to, while they had their boyfriends. Still, we got on well together and parted with all bills – phone, etc. – properly shared out.

For the third year I opted to spend my "year out" with the Intermediate Technology organisation, founded by Ernst Schumacher. His "Small is Beautiful" approach appealed to me, though my actual experience was not quite what I expected. My first thoughts had been about helping the overseas branch of the organisation, but since this seemed to be impractical I joined the home unit, located in an LEC warehouse at Elephant & Castle, London. Here I spent my time experimenting with an elementary machine that turned newspapers mixed with water into pulp, which it then pressed through rollers into sheets of cardboard-like material. This, when dried, could be formed into such things as egg-cartons – or, with my experiments, large plant-holders or laminated sheets containing flowers, seeds etc., using peat. This was the subject of the dissertation I prepared at the end of my time with ITDG.

I had now reached my fourth and final year and found accommodation with a Cypriot family near my previous digs. What a start, though.

I'd just parked the car outside while I transferred my belongings into the house: this took two or three trips. It was on the second that I heard screams of "Murder! Murder!" from the lady of the house. Dashing back in, I learned that she had just heard that her niece was with her husband - both Cypriots - when he was attacked and killed while in their hotel room. I can't remember where. Anyway, it turned into quite a mystery, where in due course there was a strong suspicion that the niece was involved with the murderer. She stayed in the house with her little girl while I was there, before the trial, the outcome of which escapes me. Unfortunately, though, I think she got off!

Apart from the frantic cries, it was a noisy house, for as is typical of people from that part of the world, the TV was on at almost full blast for most of the day and evening. I bought earplugs and used my headphones in an attempt to have some peace to study. I left here for home early in March, '85 when I got word that our Mother was seriously ill in the ERI. Sadly, she died before I left Maidenhead to visit her. On my return from Edinburgh and the funeral I commuted by car to the Poly for the remaining weeks, until the final exams were over.

Looking back more than 25 years later as I write this particular excerpt, the four years spent at the Poly was an experience I'm glad I had and this though achieving a modest 2/2 to gain my BSc (Hons) in Society & Technology and a Diploma of Education. All were hard-earned, though easier, perhaps, than deserved. The aims of the course were to get one to be able to appreciate the approach of science and technology to society and vice versa. So philosophy and technological history were studied, and to reach this level one had to show certain prowess in physics, chemistry and maths etc. Not easy for a 62-year-old, as I was on graduating.

In the meantime Ann had been teaching English full-time at Maidenhead College, and Moira was working in London as a technical translator. Sarah was about to leave school after her A-levels to start a degree course in Edinburgh. So endeth one major episode - and on to the next – the great move North!
In March '82 Maggie Macaskill, of Kyle View, Kyleakin, auntie of Ann, died, leaving the house to be shared between Ann, Moira and Sarah. We went to her funeral in Broadford while staying in a self-catering croft-house in Teangue, Sleat. Later that summer Ann and Sarah spent time in Kyle View tidying up to get it ready for renting as a self-catering place. Because of its poor condition not much was charged but those who responded were delighted with their stay. We planned to take over the house ourselves in the summer of '85, once Ann and Sarah had finished with their schools and I, as mentioned, had left the Poly.

We'd lived in our Maidenhead house for 17 years, Moira since she was ten and Sarah from one year, when we put it up for sale, so the prospect of saying goodbye to it wasn't what everyone looked forward to. Neither Ann nor myself were too reluctant, for the pull of Skye was a large plus in favour of the move. But for the girls the parting from life-long friends and associations were much harder to bear.

In September '85, after some delay caused by the purchaser, we upped sticks and headed for Skye, £67,000 to the good, less the real-estate agent's fees, of course, and a house awaiting us which came free – and yet – Kyle View was in quite a state of disrepair so that by the time the roof and windows had been replaced, the floors covered with boards or vinyl tiles, the outside walls stripped and replastered and the old kitchen demolished to make way for the present one, the bathroom furniture replaced and a downstairs toilet and shower installed, not much remained of the money left in the bank. Still, we did have enough to buy a one-bedroom flat in Forest Hill, Edinburgh, thinking that it would be of use for Sarah while at University. It was used by both girls at different times but once these finished and there were calls by neighbours to contribute to building repairs, plus the hassle with the rates and taxes, we decided to sell it. Looking back, this was a bit short-sighted, perhaps, since had we kept it we might have had a return of three or four more times what we'd sold it for in the 80s (£32,000, the same as we paid for it).

However, our arrival at Kyle View was followed by the furniture van with all our then worldly goods. I say then because we inherited from Auntie Maggie so many chairs, chests of drawers, beds and small tables that we were overwhelmed and out of space to contain everything. Many of these items we sold.

There were six leather-covered dining chairs which had apparently graced the bottoms of many distinguished persons at Kyle House in years past. Maggie had bought them during a change of ownership of the House, we understood from a neighbour, Nella McRae, who had worked there as a girl.

Going back to expenditure on Kyle View, there was the re-wiring and installing of 13-amp sockets throughout in place of the outdated 15-amp round-plug versions, plus a central-heating system consisting of a multi-fuel stove with a back boiler for heating the water stored in a tank in the loft. An immersion heater was switched on when the stove wasn't in use. After about 7 years we replaced this system with a combination boiler fuelled by liquid petroleum gas (LPG) as supplied by Calor. However, 16 years later, because the boiler was failing, we applied for and were granted a completely new system under the Government's central heating scheme for pensioners. This resulted in the removal of the boiler and the nine radiators, which were replaced by four storage heaters, two panel heaters and a Megaflow cylinder for hot water, all free of charge! I shouldn't think there will be any need for a further change in my time. If so, I'll let you know.

The beauty of having the hot water storage tank removed from the loft was the space it allowed for a comfortable bedroom and not the cramped area as before. In any event the acidic water in the tank at that time burned a hole in it and it leaked onto the squeezed-in bed holding a much-perturbed Sarah. Our water is no longer the brown peaty stuff provided from a local source on the Kylerhea road. The completion of the bridge meant that supplies of clean, filtered water are now brought across from a source outside Kyle.

Another advantage since we came was the installation of a sewerage system to replace the Obbe as a repository. Prior to this one waited between tides of this tidal inlet before flushing the toilet. Recently the system became even more sophisticated when the Water Board put in a treatment system which can be seen on the approach to Kyle House.

I seem to be jumping ahead a bit, but having lived in Kyleakin for more than 25 years, it's a bit difficult, not to mention uninteresting, to describe events in strictly chronological order.

As can be imagined, the first year to 18 months of our arrival at Kyle View was quite chaotic. Not only did we have an excess of furniture but we were all but overwhelmed by joiners, slaters, plumbers and stonemasons as they more or less jointly carried out their tasks. The work was behind what we had anticipated, which led to some embarrassment.

Ann had seen an advert somewhere, where a Swiss family of parents and two small boys wanted accommodation for a number of weeks in Scotland, combined with tuition in English. So on top of the problems of unfinished work we had father Patrick, mother Jeannette, four-year-old Sebastian and his little brother descend on us. But fortunately, despite the shortcomings, they were very tolerant and obviously enjoyed their stay. Patrick was well over six feet and from a German canton, while his wife was of average height and from the French-speaking canton, with all speaking Italian since they lived in an Italian canton. The parents could converse adequately enough in English to be understood. Ann was now in her element and held sessions daily, two hours at a time, teaching the language to each parent individually.

Patrick was keen on fishing but not having a car relied on me to take him and the boys to the Lusa river beside the Kylerhea road. On one occasion Tuppy, our dear old collie, stayed with them while I drove off home. Sometime later a man came to the door saying he'd seen a dog that looked like ours making its way along the main road towards the village. Sure enough, she'd walked most of the way back when I met her, a distance of 3 or 4 miles. We kept in touch with the family for a few years afterwards. Another Swiss family visited later but by this time the house was in order, more or less. I can't remember much about them, though.

It was about this time, towards the end of the 80s, that we decided to do Bed & Breakfast and did so until the end of the 90s, when certain changes took place in the village which put us off, not to mention the strain put on Ann in particular, with our advancing years. The pubs became licenced to stay open until 1 am, with the result that some residents, usually Aussie girls, would crawl into the house about 2 am. Some, including older men, would smoke in their bedrooms. One Scots girl did, in fact, burn a hole in a duvet cover without telling us before she left. I must say, though, that the majority of those staying with us over the years were friendly, and showed their appreciation, as evidenced in the Visitors' Books we hold.

As I write, the whole concept of B&B has changed. Where dozens of backpackers and more sophisticated visitors would wander around looking for a place to stay overnight and not always successfully, the Youth Hostel, formerly the Marine Hotel, and in time a number of private hostels opened up to accommodate them. Then, because of demand, B&Bs found that potential customers were becoming more sophisticated and wanted places providing en suite rooms. Owners had to adjust accordingly but at a cost. Also, in time the B&B owners had their own websites, so that bookings are now made electronically and only a few visitors knock on doors. In 2008, the Youth Hostel closed down, thus reducing bed places by 120, to add to those lost when the Haggis Backpackers outfit from Edinburgh left Kyleakin. The outcome was a small village rapidly losing another source of income.

Later in 2008 we received a copy of an outline planning application from the Skye & Lochalsh Housing Association to convert the hostel into something like 15 flats and ground-floor space for community use. Planning permission was granted in March 2009 and by early September 2011 the former hostel had been converted into 12 flats.

Also in 2008 some villagers decided to form the Kyleakin & Kylerhea Community Company, set up to try and highlight the growing problem of the decline of business in the area. It is quite disturbing to review the losses to the village since 1995, for example. Not only were 120 beds lost from the hostel but other things, such as showers and toilet facilities for visitors to the Marina, as well as laundry and drying aids for boat crews.

There used to be a chip shop, a bakery, a woollens shop, places for hiring mopeds and cycles, a village-based taxi hire service, an Internet station in the hostel and, perhaps the biggest change, which impinged on many of these, usually resulting in their demise, was the closing down of the ferry with the loss of 35 local jobs. Certainly, having the bridge has been good for the island as a whole, especially now that it is toll-free, but there is little doubt that without the ferry and the visitors it brought the village has been severely disadvantaged.

On the plus side, the villagers have benefited because of the bridge, through improved pavements, street lighting and water supplies, now that it is piped from the mainland via the bridge. No longer is one's bath full of peaty brown liquid with bits in it from its source on the road to Kylerhea. These benefits come at a cost, of course: because Kyle View is assessed under the Council Tax system as band E, water and waste water cost us a total of £400 plus per year, while the total Council Tax is £1902, quite a chunk out of our pensions.

In 1998 I answered an ad in the local paper by a couple from Cape Cod wanting to exchange houses for a month. This seemed to be an ideal opportunity to spend time with Moira and her family, who were living in Boston at the time. The strange thing is that despite many exchanges of notes, letters and cards, we never actually met Bruce MacKenzie and his partner, although we might have met a couple of years ago when we were invited to holiday with them at the flat they own in the South of France. Tempted though we were, it was felt that I wasn't quite up to gadding about without imposing on them for getting around sight-seeing. Bruce is only a couple of years younger than me. So we declined, which was a shame, because Ann had always been keen to visit France.

The house in Orleans had been a ten-room restaurant in former days while belonging to Bruce's parents. Many well-known U.S.

political figures were said to have taken tea here over the years, starting in the 19th century. The house stood alone in extensive grounds with plenty of grass and trees to relax in. Part of the deal included an exchange of cars. This was hilarious, for Bruce's car, an ancient Mercedes with around 200,000 miles on the clock, diesel and left-hand drive, of course, faced us with a challenge. Getting started was one thing, with smoke pouring out of the exhaust once the engine had fired, much to the chagrin of Ann, who would be at the back guiding me on to the road. She wasn't pleased. The fact that the speedometer didn't work was another trying factor. However, we did manage to see most of Cape Cod but kept well clear of Boston. It was a very enjoyable holiday and equally so for Bruce and partner, who had the use of our Micra, much newer but considerably smaller.

Bruce had gone to West Point as a boy but I can't remember what he did from then onwards except that he seemed to have something to do with the Peace Corps and that his car had taken him around many countries in Europe, Africa etc.

This was not our only exchange, for earlier, in 1994, we swapped with a couple, Jack and Karen Whittle, from Calgary, Alberta. He was an Edinburgh chap who'd worked with U.K. Post Office Telephones and had just retired from the local telephone company where he'd worked for a number of years.

Theirs was a nicely appointed house on Elbow Drive, parallel to the Elbow River and near to a trail used by walkers, joggers and cyclists. It was on this trail that I came a cropper, as I will reveal later, an event which, in a way, clouded our stay.

We also exchanged cars, his being a second-hand, five-year-old Saab – in beautiful condition; ours was a Micra 1.2 – a bit smaller, of course. The double garage had double doors, which had us a bit baffled at first, for although they opened and closed automatically, there was some knack to it which I can't remember, though after a while it seemed simple enough. There were his & her bikes in the garage and despite our lack of practice we thought, with the day being so nice, we'd pack sandwiches and go for a cycle on the leisure trail. This was only a few days after our arrival and we hadn't dared take the car out yet.

Spinning along merrily, we arrived at a steep incline, dismounted and walked up. Stopping a few yards later, we sat and ate our sandwiches, then headed back to the house and tragedy.

I was cycling closely behind Ann and when she stopped suddenly at the top of the incline, being fearful of going down it, I braked. Normally I would have dismounted by throwing my leg over but there wasn't time, nor could I straddle the bar because the bike was too big for me. So I put my left foot on the ground and, after staggering a bit, fell down on my left side. I knew instantly that I was injured, but not by how much.

Fortunately, there were people using the trail while on their lunch-break and one chap used his mobile to call 999 or the equivalent. Within a few minutes a police car arrived, followed by an ambulance, and the paramedics put me on oxygen, then went on to Bayview Hospital, uncertain whether my leg was bruised or broken. X-rays showed a fracture of my femur requiring a metal plate and ten pins to hold it together. The wound was stapled and after 8 days I was discharged. Fortunately the large financial cost for this - £8000 - was covered by insurance. But what of poor Ann, left alone after only a few days in a strange city? The policeman came to her aid by taking her and the bikes back to the house – much appreciated.

Next day the brave soul!! managed somehow to open the garage doors, start the car and drive it to the hospital. This was some achievement: a strange car, quite big, left-hand drive and unaccustomed controls, driving on the "wrong" side of the road in traffic to a place of whose position she had only a vague idea. If ever there was one occasion when a Conspicuous Gallantry Award was earned, this was it. She was to make more visits until the final one when I was discharged on crutches.

Although we were only two weeks or so into our 8-week holiday, my mishap proved not to be such a drag as may have been expected, for after a few days I found that I was able to drive without discomfort or damage to my wound or to the public. Anyway, that's how it turned out. With lovely weather, first-class library near at hand and a comfortable place at the rear of the house where one could relax with a book, a cigar and maybe a glass of wine, there was no need to venture out in the car that much. We did, however, spend a week-end at Lake Louise in the Rockies, visiting Banff on the way. We stayed in a hotel that was usually a venue for skiers but was fairly quiet, it being out of season. This seemed obvious, for I was the only one on crutches! It was here that we saw a wolf. It crossed the road in front of us and on reaching the verge turned its head towards us casually, not in the least perturbed. Safely in the car, neither were we, although we wished we'd had the camera handy.

Another trip was to the Badlands, an extensive area of open country and a fruitful area for dinosaur fossils. We visited the museum with many of these on display. On leaving there we came to a township and saw a sign for B&B. This was on a farm and we spent the night in a tidy little chalet a few hundred yards from the farmhouse. The farmer's wife was a very pleasant and good-looking young woman who served us fruit for breakfast, quite a change from the customary bacon and eggs etc. We were quite far away from Calgary, on the road north to Edmonton.

Back in the city we went to the Calgary and Glenbow Museum, where we learned that a certain James Macleod from Gesto House in Skye named the place after Calgary Bay in Mull where, as a boy, he spent summer holidays with his parents. His predecessor, a Frenchman, had given the place a French name without official approval.

James Macleod (b. 1836, d. 1894) had a distinguished career. He was a lawyer, soldier, judge and Commissioner of the NorthWest Mounted Police. He established Fort Macleod and suppressed the trade of whisky with the Indians.

We thoroughly enjoyed this exchange holiday, not realising we'd be having another just 7 months later.

It was soon after our arrival home that a couple wrote saying how they would like to exchange with us for 3 weeks in May: they lived in Amsterdam. We were only too willing and met at Turnhouse Airport on their arrival and our departure. No cars exchanged this time nor, strangely enough for Holland, bikes.

The house was typical of the city, tall and narrow, with all the rooms one on top of the other, none side by side. The man was a professor and his wife also an academic. A car wasn't necessary, the public transport of trams, buses and rail being excellent and inexpensive. Apart from visits to the usual tourist centres, art galleries etc., we did a more or less round trip of the country by train, dropping off at places such as Arnhem, Groningen and Venlo.

Both Moira and Ann's sister Chris stayed with us for a few days, though not at the same time. It was good to have their company visiting art galleries and on a train journey to Rotterdam.

When Sarah graduated from Edinburgh University in 1989 she followed up her English degree with a course in Teaching English as a Foreign Language in London. Given the choice of countries to teach in, she chose Turkey. Normally TEFL teachers stay in their chosen country for a year or so but, as with others, Sarah remains until this day, as I write. She married Turkish mining engineer Sami, with whom she has three sons and a daughter. We attended their marriage in 1991, a civil ceremony in a council-like building with an imam in charge, in Sami's home town of Konya, a very conservative type of place. Also while staying there we had the privilege of watching a performance by The Whirling Dervishes in the presence of Turkey's president. Ann and I, and later Moira, stayed with Sami's parents, Kamil and Hacer, throughout our visit and were overcome by their hospitality. I did feel a bit let down on the eve of the wedding, though.

The custom was for the females to congregate in one room of the house and the males in the other. There must have been 15 to 20 men sitting in chairs against the walls sipping tea in the usual small glasses. I thought this was just the prelude to something stronger coming up; after all I could see bottles of whisky, etc. lying on a corner shelf. The time passed with more tea being served but nothing stronger. And such was the case then and on later visits. They are all practising Moslems, of course, Sami being an exception. However, I had the feeling that attendance at the mosque could be compared to pre-war Scotland (1939-45). But where church-going in Scotland has since dried up massively, such is not the case in Turkey.

After the wedding we went to Alanya, a resort by the Med. Being the month of June it was so hot that you couldn't walk on bare feet on the beach. This was a place popular with Germans, so much so that food stores and restaurants catered for them, with menus and notices being mainly in German.

Other trips in Turkey took us to Anatolia, to Gallipoli and to Troy, all by buses which, on the whole, are cheap and comfortable. We found the small hotels we stayed at the same. Our final visit to this great and varied country was at Christmas, 2000.

With Kamil and his cousins at the site of the oldest town in the world

These days our highlight of the year is in July/August when Sarah and the children arrive from Istanbul for a 3-4 week stay. In 1992 she brought four-month-old Tan and in 1996 Teoman was added when he was eight months. Tolga was born in situ, as it were, in Raigmore Hospital in July 2001. Last of all came their wee sister Aylin in 2008. Sami has also come a couple of times but his visits are limited by work pressures. We have one or two video-tapes taken during some of their visits. A large bonus for us was the decision by Moira and Kevin to leave Boston, Mass. and come to live on Skye.

The grandchildren in Kyle View 2008

Kevin and me supervising Tolga's birthday party

During our time here in Kyleakin I became involved in a number of activities over and above working in the house and in the garden, which was quite a jungle on our arrival. I dug, levelled and seeded all the grass areas on view now. The other parts had to be cleared of ground elder – with Roundup – and brambles. A previous cutting of the hedge had left large branches on the ground which needed clearing, while veronica had grown massively, stretching all the way to the path leading from the front door. Later, when we came back from Amsterdam in May, '95, I had to cope with massively high grass on all the lawns, with a sickle, not the scythe I'd lent to my friend John Macleod a few years earlier. Sadly, John died in '94 and his niece disposed of the scythe along with the other contents of the house. We had enjoyed many drams together in the years before, having inherited him from Ann's Auntie Maggie.

We'd been here for only a few months when I was inveigled by Cathie Grant to attend a practice of the Strath Gaelic Choir. I remained with them for the following five years, in three of which I was Treasurer. Ann had known Catherine, as she did a number of the locals, from her earlier days on the island.

Despite my lack of Gaelic, I managed to hold my position as a tenor at five Mods and various concerts without creating any major embarrassment, though there were a few giggles at my pronunciation occasionally. I had every reason going to become reasonably proficient in the language, especially since Ann as a native speaker was willing and did help me – but I feel that at aged 60 it was too late. My brain hadn't got over the pounding it took during the four years at Middlesex University. Even before joining the choir I had attended a 2-week learning course at Sabhal Mòr Ostaig, Skye's Gaelic College, but that didn't help.

The Mods, or Whisky Olympics, as they're called for obvious reasons, took place in a different venue each year in October. I attended Stirling, Glasgow (twice), Stornoway and finally Dingwall in 1993, I think. We'd travel by hired bus and stay at hotels or B&B, depending on the availability because of the hundreds of participants from all over the country. As a choir we did well some years, lifting trophies, or were barren others. It could be good fun during the evenings after the competition with gatherings in hotels or other places we stayed in. There was plenty of music, fuelled by varying amounts of whisky during these sessions. It was a time too when friends from other parts came together for another year.

There was an unwritten code observed by the Strath Choir at least and that was never to carry back to Kyleakin any misdemeanours by any of the members. I'm pleased to record my not having been aware of any happenings that anyone might have been ashamed of.

Following an election for the Kyleakin & Kylerhea Community Council, I joined eight others as Councillors. I was proposed as Chairman but I declined because in my experience this was an inactive post, that of Secretary being the one engaging with the day-to-day activities, whereby one conveyed in writing to the appropriate authorities the conclusions of one's fellow councillors. This, however, was not the tradition of the council: it was the chairman who had this responsibility, which I found most frustrating. I did manage to write letters which resulted in repairs to the Fishermen's Pier, long neglected, and the removal of a wooden hulk which had been laid up in the Obbe and was a hazard to children playing on it. Also, using the penny fund, an accumulation from the rates for special unscheduled work, I convinced the Transport Officer to tarmac the road, King Street, which is reached from behind the Church of Scotland: it had been massively pot-holed for years.

Strath Gaelic Choir Glasgow Mod 1988
We won five out of six prizes!

For the next six years or so I was actively involved with the Skye Bridge Appeal Group, which was set up to oppose the building of the bridge. We objected among other things to the way in which it was to be funded, which included the imposition of unacceptably high tolls for all users of the bridge. I was interviewed several times for radio and TV and was part of a delegation that addressed MPs at Westminster. My involvement culminated in August, '97 with the publication of a booklet entitled "The Skye Bridge, an Unfinished Story". The West Highland Free Press published 1000 copies at a charge of £1500 which was paid for from funds donated by the Appeal Group and one donation by Clodagh MacKenzie, Kyle House, of £400. Some 300 copies were distributed free of charge by post to various politicians, the media and members of the Appeal Group in its original form. With a sale price of £3-£4, depending on the buyer, i.e. whether or not for resale, an overall profit of £735 was made. This was donated to the Kyle & Kyleakin Eilean Ban Trust, along with the balance remaining in the Appeal Group's funds, as agreed in the Constitution, which stated that such funds should be given to charity once the group was disbanded. I handed over a cheque for the total amount to Virginia McKenna of Born Free and Ring of Bright Water fame, who had led the campaign to have the island and the lighthouse put into the trust of the local community, at a formal opening of the Brightwater Centre in Spring, 2000.

The secretary of the Appeal Group was Pam Noble. She contributed greatly to the booklet as those who have a copy of it can see. And spent many hours of her time conveying the decisions of the Group to the public and diverse authorities over the seven years of its existence.

Alongside Pam and me, the chairman, was the late Kathleen Macrae, who did an excellent job as treasurer and as a most coherent spokesperson, and Cathy Reid, our able Gaelic communicator.

There was a film on TV recently which portrayed the 'heroes' of the protests against the bridge tolls as being the members of the Skye And Kyle Against Tolls (SKAT) organisation with no mention of the part played by the Skye Bridge Appeal Group. This was obviously a deliberate lack of balance by the producer in favour of the excitement, colour and drama provided by the stories of those who were arrested and fined for refusing to pay the toll, one of whom landed in jail for what was assessed as a criminal act.

The methods employed by SKAT certainly drew a great deal of attention to the controversy, despite the fact that as an organisation it only came to life on the eve of the bridge's opening to traffic.

The Appeal Group, however, was formed before the bridge was even built. Our approach was one of written and verbal protest to the media and politicians and our tasks included keeping the many other group members up to date with developments. We had MPs Brian Wilson and Charles Kennedy as patrons. And while the former no doubt influenced his boss Donald Dewar to reduce the tolls when he became First Minister of the Scottish Parliament in 1997, it was Lib. Dem. Charles Kennedy and his fellow party members, whether in Edinburgh or Westminster, whose constant pressure led to the removal of the tolls. Tavish Scott, the Lib. Dem. MSP, was Transport Minister in the Labour/Lib. Dem. coalition government; following the buyout of Inverness Airport, a victim of the Private Finance Initiative (PFI), he negotiated the buyout of the bridge from the Bank of America at a scandalous cost.

The acrimony, rage and "criminality" surrounding the introduction of the bridge need not have happened had the

Conservative government not been so anxious to introduce the principle of PFI into Scotland before the 1992 General Election, which the polls indicated it would lose. The bridge must have been seen as a soft choice with little likelihood of opposition from this fringe, low-population community, many of whom would welcome its arrival - which they did, until they learned of the iniquitous tolls regime.

Had there been a moratorium of only a few months, the likelihood is that with Objective 1, the European Union initiative which provided funding for projects like the bridge in the Highlands and Islands, there could have been a bridge free of tolls, which would have conformed with Highland Council's original policy. However, because work had begun before the opening date for applications, the Skye Bridge lost out. Still, since the prohibitive tolls were eventually scrapped, we have come to appreciate the bridge as the asset that it is.

On the terrace of the House of Commons with Ian Begg -1996

SKAT and Appeal Group joint delegation to Westminster June 1996, sponsored by Charles Kennedy MP

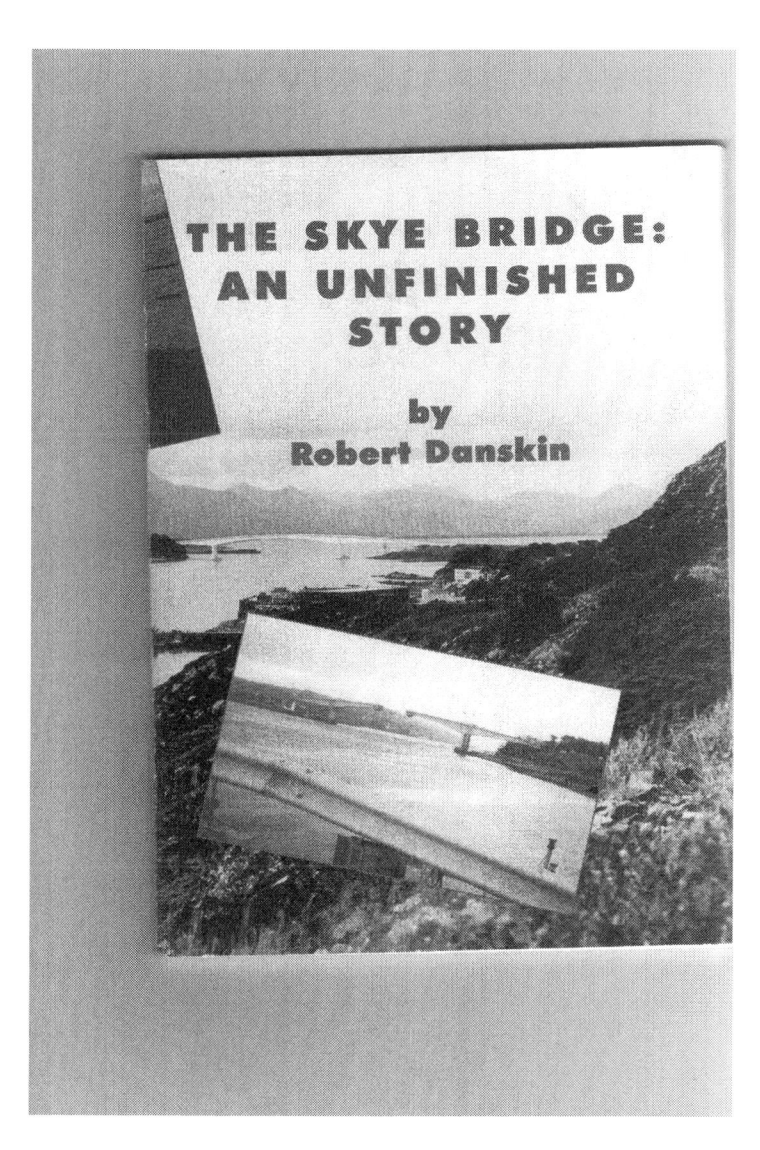

*The booklet showing developments leading
to the ending of tolls*

The Vision

1. To make safe access to the island by sea from Kyleakin.
2. To restore the buildings as a home for a permanent warden.
3. To clear the way for paths leading from the landing to designated areas on the island.
4. To upgrade the appearance of the ground surrounding the buildings by a measure of landscaping.
5. To install CCTV cameras to strategic points related to the flora and fauna and to relay the pictures to a screen(s) in an interpretive centre at a location in Kyleakin.
6. To invite specialists in their field to guide and instruct those visitors interested in the flora and fauna of the island.
7. To encourage businesses and others to contribute to the upkeep of the Trust.
8. To respect the sensitive nature of the island and safeguard its natural heritage for many years to come.

A Kyleakin/Kyle and The Born Free Foundation
COMMUNITY PARTNERSHIP

The Lighthouse

Kyleakin Lighthouse was built from brick and stone and shone its first light from the 7th house in 1857. There were two keepers housed with their families in the two cottages later occupied by Gavin Maxwell into one. The keepers' children went to school in Kyleakin.

In 1960 the lighthouse became automatic and the keepers redundant, so it was in 1963 that the naturalist and author bought the cottages.

Note: Kyleakin Lighthouse Island: A Short History by C.S. Knighton, printed in 1982 by The West Highland Publishing Company is well worth reading.

The Conservationist

It was Gavin Maxwell, aristocrat, SOE instructor, writer, shark hunter, poet, painter and life-long naturalist whose idea it was to make Eilean Bàn a wild-life park. This followed the catastrophe at Sandaig, Camusfeàrna when the house was destroyed by fire and with it his possessions, and one of his favourite otters – Edal.

Apart from creating a colony of diverse animals such as otters, St Kilda sheep, foxes, deer, wild goats and a variety of predatory birds, he planned to increase the numbers of breeding eider ducks to the level where the amount of down produced would make the effort a commercially viable proposition.

Sadly, his ambitions for the island came to nought when he died in 1969 at the early age of 55 years.

Among his many books, "Ring of Bright Water" and the film of that name gave Maxwell international acclaim and money for his projects.

Among the books covering aspects of his life "Gavin Maxwell – A Life" by Douglas Botting would seem to be the most comprehensive.

196

TO ALL RESIDENTS OF KYLEAKIN/KYLERHEA AND KYLE AND THEIR FAMILIES

The 17th October, 1998 is a historic date for the communities of Kyleakin, Kylerhea and Kyle, for it i on this day that Eilean Ban will be transferred from the ownership of The Scottish Office to a Trust, th trustees of which will be representatives of the two villages and The Born Free Foundation.

When it became known after the completion of the Skye Bridge that the island had been put up fc auction in Glasgow, the alarm was raised and fears expressed about the consequences to the Island' wild-life now that access is readily available from the bridge. Fortunately, as the result of pleas to Th Scottish Office by The Born Free Foundation, the sale was cancelled.

It was from this point that the work to justify the claim for transfer of ownership to a community-le Trust, consisting of the villagers and The Born Free Foundation, got under way. And it is thanks to th dedicated efforts of those who gave voluntarily of their expertise in the fields of accountancy, th environment and other disciplines that Eilean Ban was given Trustee status at such an early date.

The members of the Community Councils and the BFF, who transmitted their enthusiasm for th project to the Scottish Office Roads Directorate, Highland Council, Highland and Islands Enterprise Northern Lighthouse Board, The National Trust for Scotland and International Otter Survival Fund ar also to be commended. The support given by these bodies has been substantial, whether by funding by the provision of other resources or by expert advice, and it is hoped that this will continue alon with contributions from other sources. The success of the project will depend on you and you neighbours and on others outside the community.

With all the interest and goodwill generated by the Project, it seems certain that this unique Proje can continue to bring wildlife and people together in a positive way, that can only benefit both fc generations to follow.

The Project

- To retain ownership of Eilean Ban within the Kyleakin and Kyle community to their mutua benefit, in partnership with The Born Free Foundation.
- To conserve and enhance the island's flora and fauna.
- To provide an educational environment, as well as a place worth visiting for its historic pas The Eilean Ban Experience aims to allow people of **all** abilities the opportunity to sympathetically appreciate the abundant wildlife on and around the island.

Eilean Ban Gala Day

A celebration will be held on Kyleakin green at 1.00pm on Saturday 17th October 1998, t which all villagers are invited.

Planned activities:

- Formal hand-over of Eilean Ban and the Lighthouse
- Workshops and displays being held throughout the day in both Kyle and Kyleakin
- A barbecue to be held in Kyle during the evening (weather permitting)
- Opportunities to volunteer your services in furthering the development of the Project

WE LOOK FORWARD TO SEEING YOU THERE AND JOINING IN THE CELEBRATIONS!!

BORN FREE

ADDRESS
Born Free Foundation
3 Grove House Foundry Lane
Horsham West Sussex
RH13 5PL England

TELEPHONE
01403 240170

FACSIMILE
01403 327838

E-MAIL
wildlife@bornfree.org.uk

WEB SITE
http://www.bornfree.org.uk

CHIEF EXECUTIVE
William Travers

BORN FREE FOUNDATION PROJECTS
BIG CAT PROJECT
ELEFRIENDS PROJECT
ORCA PROJECT
PRIMATE PROJECT
UK WILDLIFE PROJECT
WOLF PROJECT
ZOO CHECK PROJECT

TRUSTEES
Virginia McKenna
Joanna Lumley OBE
Terry Dickinson Monty Ruben
Rachael Heyman Rupert Grey
Terry Adams Simon Trevor

The charity is a charitable
company limited by guarantee
Charity Registration No 1070906
Company Registration No 03603432
VAT No 528340551

2nd November 1998

Bob Danskin Esq.
Kyle View
Kyleakin
Isle of Skye

Dear Bob,

We met briefly on October 17th but I don't think I really thanked you for not only designing but funding the Eilean Ban information leaflet.

It was marvellous of you and the leaflet was excellent.

Now the project is launched and work really begins.   There's a lot to do before April!

I look forward to seeing you again.

All good wishes

Yours sincerely,

Virginia

Virginia McKenna

BORN FREE

address
born free foundation
3 grove house foundry lane
horsham west sussex
rh13 5pl uk

telephone
01403 240170

facsimile
01403 327838

email
wildlife@bornfree.org.uk

website
www.bornfree.org.uk

chief executive officer
william travers

"born free is an
international wildlife
charity working to
prevent animal suffering
and protect species
in the wild"

trustees
virginia mckenna
joanna lumley OBE
terry adams
rupert grey
rachel heyman
monty ruben
simon trevor
ronnie wilkie

the charity is a charitable
company limited by guarantee

charity no 1070906

Mr. Bob Danskin
Kyle View
Kyleakin
Isle of Skye IV41
Scotland

6 June 2000

Dear Mr. Danskin

My apologies for the delay in writing to thank The Skye Bridge Appeal Group for the very generous cheque you presented to me for the Eilean Ban Trust on May 19th. It was the most wonderful surprise and I am sure you realise how grateful we all are.

It was a really happy day – warmth from the crowds who were there, and from the sun! How lucky we were.

Please convey my thanks to your colleagues.

All good wishes

Yours sincerely

Virginia McKenna

Virginia McKenna

A cutting from the Guardian dated 29th August 2012

Similarly, the 1969 film adaptation of Gavin Maxwell's Ring of Bright Water, which also starred both McKenna and Travers, motivated her to get involved in saving Maxwell's house on Eilean Ban, near Skye. Together with local people, she helped form the Eilean Ban Trust. "I was given the responsibility to recreate his large sitting room," she says enthusiastically. "So armed with photographs and stories from people who knew him, I toured antique shops to find things that resembled, as near as possible, artefacts in the room. I bought from various friends and acquaintances, things that were in the room, like the sofa and table. It was the most fascinating job to do, wonderful. It took many months."

She adds: "It was a great privilege because I stayed on the island a few times. People said 'aren't you scared because there are ghosts'. I must admit I never heard any of those things, but I did see otters and seals. It was just absolute magic."

Ann and I celebrated our 56th Wedding Anniversary in May 2013 and as the song goes 'it don't seem a day too much'. We have weathered the years together and benefited from having two lovely daughters who between them have produced six grandchildren whose growing up has given us much pleasure. Now that my mobility is somewhat impaired it has fallen upon Ann to do the mundane household tasks I`d normally perform - using a screw driver and changing light bulbs, for example, and she does them beautifully. I made a fortunate choice all these years ago and long may our partnership continue.

When my Father first met Ann he said to me afterwards she'd be safe as the Bank of Scotland - he should have said safer!

DANSKIN GENEALOGY

The following letter inspired my Father and my cousin Joe Danskin to compile their own family trees once they had complied as best they could with the writer's request:

                       1810 Cedar Street,
                       Alhambra, California, U.S.A.
                       Nov. 11, 1955

Dear Mr. Danskin;

    The purpose of this letter is to obtain some information about the Danskin family of which I am a member. During the past few months I have been assembling data for a family 'tree' of the Danskin family which left Scotland in 1829 for Canada. Perhaps you can advise me where to inquire for some of the data I lack. I shall be very grateful for any information you may furnish.

    My great-great-grandfather, William (1746-1806), lived in Cumbernauld, Scotland. If possible I would like to trace his lineage, on the Danskin side, to an earlier date. Is there a practicable way to do this without going to a professional (and expensive) genealogist? My great-grandfather, George (1777- 1860), lived in Cumbernauld and in 1829 left Scotland for America where he settled near Huntingdon, Quebec Province, Canada. He was the father of eleven children: William (1798-1858), John (1800-1863), Thomas (1802-1832), George (1804-1888) my grandfather – an elder and preacher in the Presbyterian Church, James (1806-1881), Agnes (1808-1898), Andrew (1810-1828), Ebenezer (1811-1877), Anne (1814-1878), Alexander (1816-1908) and Gilmore (1819-1900). With the help of some Danskins in the U.S. I have been able to establish the descendants of nine of the above eleven children. But we have not succeeded in discovering what happened to the first two above – William and John. We believe they emigrated to Canada with their parents but we are not sure on that point.   Possibly one, or both, remained in Scotland and if that was the case I wonder what steps, if any, can be taken to trace their descendants.   Would the Presbyterian Church in Cumbernauld keep records that far back?   I would like to include their progeny in my ' tree' if it is possible to obtain it.

In the 'tree' I have started it is interesting to note the occupations chosen by the members of the Danskin 'clan'.   They have done their share in pioneering the wonderful developing economy of America as farmers, stockmen, mine operators and lumbermen. They appear often in the professions as lawyers, engineers and doctors.   They are represented spiritually as ministers of the Gospel with churches in the U.S. and as missionaries in foreign lands. They also engaged in such diverse vocations as educators, salesmen, railroad builders, machinists, bankers, butchers, firemen and streetcar conductors.

Last summer I met a Mr. Robert Danskin of Norwalk, California.   He told me that he was born in England and emigrated to the U.S. In 1920.   He said the Danskin name is quite common in some of the towns near the Tyne River in Northern England.   When, as a young man, he had sailed the seas as a ship's engineer he met an English Consul (of Danskin blood) who had an explanation for the origin of the name Danskin.   The story (which strangely corroborated a similar one told to me by another Danskin many years ago) is as follows:-

A Swedish prince (Johanson) led his own army as mercenaries in the service of Denmark against the Germans.   The Danes won and when Prince Johanson returned to Denmark the Danish King showered him with many favors, one of which was the bestowal of a Danish cognomen (Dan's kin or Dansken or Danskken) meaning, roughly, 'kin of the Danes'.   Many years later brothers Peter and George (descendants of Prince Johanson) joined a Norse invasion of the British Isles.   Peter remained in the Tyne River area and founded the English line.   George went to Scotland and founded our line.   The actual dates of the above events are not known.   Is this story fact or fancy?   Or a mixture of both?   If you have any knowledge of the above account I would appreciate receiving your version – including dates if known.   It makes a good story even if not entirely true – eh?

      Sincerely,
      JOHN MOFFAT DANSKIN

My Father and Joe went to the church in Cumbernauld where they were able to confirm it was one of William's (1746-1806) sons, George, who had emigrated to Canada with his wife and eleven children.

Meanwhile, J.M.D. had been compiling his Family Tree, a copy of which he sent to my Father. It is a very interesting document - so much so that one wonders how George could have had so many descendants in such a relatively short period – not much more than 100 years.

I find the details of three of these particularly unique. There was Asa Danskin, killed in the San Franscisco earthquake in 1906. While Wm. Danskin (1850-1912) was married to a niece of Abraham Lincoln, the President. The following is an excerpt from the book *Indian Wars of the West* by A.J. Bledsoe, published in 1885 in San Franscisco, describing the killing by Indians of members of a Danskin family:

CHAPTER XXV.

DABY'S FERRY

A Night of Terror. - Adventures of a heroic Woman. - Mrs. Danskin's fate. - Babes in the Wood. - Peter Nizet and George Danskin.

Five miles North of Union, where the main road crossed Mad River, a settler, S. Daby, had established a ferry and located Government land. The house was a stopping-place for travelers, well patronized, and the ferry property produced a handsome income. The surrounding neighborhood was not thickly settled. The ferry-house was situated in a wild spot not far from the gloomy forests. Daby himself saw the advantages which were certain to accrue from an early settlement there, for he knew that the land, when once cleared and under cultivation, would be remarkably productive. The Government price was exceedingly low. He could afford to wait for increase of values and profits.

Supper was on the table at the Daby House at 6 o'clock on the evening of June 6th, 1862. Around the board gathered Mr. Daby and his wife, their three children, Mrs. Danskin, mother of Mrs. Daby, and a boy, George Danskin, Mrs. Daby's nephew. In a tent near the house were two soldiers from Camp Gaston, and on the place were also a Frenchman named Peter Nizet and a half-breed Indian boy. Nizet, who took his meals with the family, had not come in. Mr. Daby went to the door and called Nizet. As he did so a bullet whistled by him. Other shots were heard. Hastily closing the door, Daby said the Indians were firing at the house, and told the women and children to get under the bed in Mrs. Daby's room. The back part of the house being built into a bank, and the bedroom being next to it, the retreat was a safe one so long as the house was not invaded. Mrs. Daby, Mrs. Danskin and the four children were in the bedroom a quarter of an hour, when Mr. Daby told them that their only prospect of escape was to run for the river. A trail led from the house to the river bank where

206

the canoes were tied. The winter flood had carried the ferryboat away. The inmates of the house and the two soldiers in the tent ran together towards the river. Mr. Daby had one child, Peter Nizet had one, and Mrs. Daby had the 13-months-old baby in her arms. Before reaching the river one of the soldiers was shot. Twenty guns were flashing in the gathering dusk of the evening, and bullets were flying through the air in every direction. There were Indians on both sides of the river. Exposed to a murderous cross-fire, with the prospect of escape dwindling into hopeless nothingness, the men and women and children leaped into a canoe and pushed out into the stream. From the opposite bank sounded the report of fire-arms. A fusilade of shot splashed in the water as the boat drifted with the current. Mrs. Danskin was struck by a bullet and slightly wounded. Not far down the river was a thicket of bushes. Mr. Daby suggested that a landing be made there and the party separate in the brush, for none could be saved if they continued in the canoe. The suggestion was followed, and the canoe landed. Mrs. Danskin went a few steps and fell, pierced by two bullets. Mrs. Daby, with the baby in her arms, had gone a short distance when a bullet struck her in the right arm, and she fell fainting to the ground. Although she was in a senseless condition for several minutes, she was dimly conscious of what was occurring around her. She heard her husband say to Nizet : "We will hide the children in the bushes." Then she heard no more, and when consciousness fully returned she saw nobody but Indians. She picked up her baby and started toward the clump of bushes. The Indians surrounded her and robbed her of the money and jewelry she had about her person, taking her wedding ring from her finger. Having robbed her they told her to "find papooses" and go to Union. She asked them: "Where is the little boy, George Danskin?" They answered: "Indians take the waugee boy ; you go to Arcata (Union), and send men with plenty money, and you get the waugee boy." Perceiving that the Indians did not intend to kill her or the children, she rose and went in search of the little girls. As she rose to her feet she distinctly recognized the features of two white men among the savages, imperfectly disguised as Indians, who turned quickly and walked away. When she reached the nearest thicket she heard a voice say "Mamma!" and there she found the two girls, Lizzie, aged five, and Carrie, aged three years, now the wife of C. L. M. Howard of Eureka. Carrying the baby and leading the girls, she walked two miles until she reached the forest, where, sick and weary, she hid the two girls at the foot of a tree where the dense undergrowth formed an impenetrable screen. Taking off two of her skirts, she put one under and one above the children, telling them to be still and quiet until she returned for them. Again, with her baby in her arms, she started through the woods and the fields, reaching the Prigmore farm, three miles down the river. The house was deserted. She then went back to the road, and reached the Janes' farm, where there was only a sick man named Chapman and another man who watched over him. Chapman said to his attendant : "I am not afraid to stay here alone ; you go and help Mrs. Daby to town." The man carried the baby and they started for Union. It was two o'clock in the morning. When they got to the main road they met a great crowd coming up from Union, among them a physician and Mrs. Daby's father and brothers. Mrs. Daby went on to Union, and the crowd of citizens went to the river. Mr. Daby, when the family separated at the river, had escaped unhurt, and carried the news of the attack to Union. The two soldiers also got in that night, both seriously though not fatally wounded. The relief party from Union carried the dead body of Mrs. Danskin to town at daylight. They had been unable to find the two little girls, and were about to give up the search in despair, when a fortunate idea was carried into execution by Mrs. Daby's youngest brother, John Danskin. A valuable dog belonging to the family was still on the place. John Danskin called the dog to him and said : "Jingo, go find the children!" With what seemed to the excited men as more than brute intelligence, the dog led them eagerly into the forest – and at the very spot where Mrs. Daby had left the children, stopped and growled as if directing further search. Parting the intervening boughs and brambles, the men saw the children lying there, locked in each other's arms, fast asleep.

Only Nizet, George Danskin, and the half-breed Indian boy remained to be accounted for. The half-breed was wounded in the thigh, and after a desperate fight, in which he killed two of his assailants, he escaped, crawling to Union in his disabled condition, reaching the town on Saturday night. It was the general supposition that Nizet had been killed and George Danskin carried into captivity by the Indians. Rewards were offered and searching parties organized, but with no avail. The days passed and neither Nizet or the boy was heard of. The Danskin family as a last resort employed friendly Hoopa Indians to make inquiries about the fate of Nizet and the boy, promising them a liberal reward for reliable information. At the end of nine days the Hoopa Indians returned and reported that they had ascertained the fate of the missing. The attacking Indians, they said, tried to capture the boy, but Nizet picked him up in his arms and ran to a large log which spanned the stream. Half-way across the stream Nizet was shot, falling to the water below with the boy in his arms. They fell in a deep pool, where a powerful eddy whirled them round and round and dragged them down to death. When their bodies were recovered the arms of Peter Nizet still clasped the form of the boy, loyal even in death.

It was a miraculous thing that any escaped from the river unhurt. Besides being wounded in the arm, Mrs. Daby had two bullet holes in the ruffles of her dress. There were three holes in the baby's dress. Mr. Daby had a bullet hole through his hat.

The Daby family never returned to their farm. The Indians burned the buildings and drove off the stock, and the land passed into the possession of others.

The family tree compiled by my Father is a simple production compared to the massive work of art of J.M.D. Where both started with William, the father of George, they differed in that the American tree shows the lineage of all eleven members of George's family, a massive number of descendants across the whole continent. Our tree starts with one of William's sons, also William, and, so far as I know, no similar attempt has been made to encompass his siblings.

There are only five male members of my line remaining, with no possibility of any additions, sad to say.

The name Danskin seems foreign to many people one encounters, yet according to such authorities as the New York Public Library publication *The Surnames of Scotland* by George Black, the name Dansken, Danskin or Danskine meant originally a native of Danzig (Gdansk) and can be traced to the early 17th century. It gives various examples, such as John Danskyne, a skinner in Dundee in 1616, Patrik Dansken, a constable "landwart of Craill" in 1633, while Henry Danskin was referred to King James VI by the Archbishop of St Andrews in a letter describing him as "Your Majestie's owne poet and native servant". Henry had been a contributor to the *Delitix Poetarum Scotorum* (which the King had commissioned). There are twelve Danskins in the Commissariot Record of Dunblane from 1604 onward. All in all, with the name making such an early appearance in Scotland, it should be accepted as just another Scottish name.

I feel that many people think that because the name is derived from Danzig that we are of Polish origin. The fact is that had we and our ancestors been Polish we would be Roman Catholics, whereas all the records show the Danskins here and in America to be Presbyterians. Since Danzig changed hands over the centuries between Germany and Denmark, with the name

Danzig meaning Danish Creek (Danske-vig), it is more likely that the original Danskins were citizens when one or other of these traditionally Protestant countries was in possession of the seaport.

So much for the Danskin surname, but what about the Danskin place-name?

There is a Danskine Loch and nearby farmhouse of the same name in East Lothian, but despite my many attempts to find the origins of the name in what would appear to be an unlikely location, I have been unsuccessful.

The Danskine Farmhouse

The Danskine Farmhouse is to my left

Back in 1997 I wrote to the School of Scottish Studies in Edinburgh hoping that someone there could enlighten me as to the name's origin as applied to the loch and farm. In reply, Ian A. Fraser said that the earliest reference he had is in the Register of the Great Seal of 1667, where the lands of Carfrae with their pendicles, commonly called Dansken and Middlemuir, occurs in a chapter in favour of John, Lord Hay of Yester and his wife Lady Mary Maitland. The name is also marked as Danskin on the Royal Military Survey of 1750-55.

He also writes how earlier entries for Danskin (1533) and Danskane (1550) in the same series of royal charters clearly refer to Danzig and it is likely that these were Scots versions of the Baltic seaport's name. The fact that it occurs so late in the documents suggests it was coined late, perhaps in the early 17th century. It may be a transferred name for Dawzig, but why should it be in a remote part of Lothian and a pendicle of a large estate at that? He ends by saying that the name defies derivation.

In his *Reminiscences and notices of the parishes of the county of Haddington*, John Martine relates how "Danskine inn and farm were long occupied by John Miller a well known man in his day. The inn was for a long period the halting house for travellers. Mr. Miller, it was said, knew much about the operations of the runners of contraband gin and brandy who came across the Lammermuir Hills from the Berwickshire and Northumberland coast. Dealers in such goods knew Danskine well and a supply could be got. James Craise a respectable man was also a long occupant of Danskine inn. He carried on also an extensive country husbandry implement trade. Thomas Instant was the last occupant of the inn. It has long been shut up and is now the dwelling house of Danskine farm."

There is a legend, reported in the *Berwick Advertiser* of 13/8/15, of a former landlord of the inn, a man of ferocious nature who plundered his guests and in many instances killed them. His usual practice was to allow them to proceed across the moor and pursue them on horseback with a masked face. He seems to have carried out this murderous trade without detection for years but his crimes were at last discovered by the Marquis of Tweeddale and he was handed over to justice.

Danskine Loch had its interesting time also when Oliver Cromwell and his army on their way back from Edinburgh camped at the side of it. It seems though that the ground was too soft for the heavy guns, so sheets of stone were removed from the quarry nearby and laid down as a base.

I end this chapter with two interesting observations:

From *Shetland History in the Scottish Records* I quote the following: "The Douglas Collection (GD 98) came to the Record Office in the 1930s, the bequest of an Edinburgh bookseller. One of the items it contains is an inventory of 1591, giving details of the goods taken from a great ship of `Danskene` lying in Shetland etc". This would seem to confirm that this was the name of the seaport before it became Danzig.

David Danskin (1863 – 1948) left his home in Fife in 1885 for a job with the Woolwich Arsenal Munitions factory in Kent. A year later he encouraged others to form the Arsenal Football Club of which he became captain. This famous club still exists of course and in 2012 two of David`s young descendents were paraded in front of the team's many supporters at a commemoration match. David's father, also David, was a brother of my great-grandfather James.

(The full history of David Danskin Junior can be found at http://www.burntisland.net/danskin.htm.)

Acknowledgement

This publication would not have been completed without the dedicated assistance of Moira, Tan and David and their computing skills, Ann with her editing and support from Kevin, technical and otherwise. My thanks to them all.

Printed in Great Britain
by Amazon